CLASSROOM
CULTURES

CLASSROOM CULTURES

EQUITABLE SCHOOLING FOR RACIALLY DIVERSE YOUTH

MICHELLE G. KNIGHT-MANUEL
JOANNE E. MARCIANO

FOREWORD BY H. RICHARD MILNER IV

TEACHERS COLLEGE PRESS

TEACHERS COLLEGE | COLUMBIA UNIVERSITY

NEW YORK AND LONDON

Published by Teachers College Press, 1234 Amsterdam Avenue, New York, NY 10027

Copyright © 2019 by Teachers College, Columbia University

Cover photo by Marco de Waal / Getty Images.

Library of Congress Cataloging-in-Publication Data is available at loc.gov

ISBN 978-0-8077-5956-1 (paper)
ISBN 978-0-8077-7737-4 (ebook)

Printed on acid-free paper
Manufactured in the United States of America

26   25   24   23   22   21   20   19   8   7   6   5   4   3   2   1

For all of the educators we learned with and from
while seeking more-equitable schooling

Contents

Foreword

Building on the germinal scholarship of Gloria Ladson-Billings (2009), teachers across sociopolitical contexts practice what Michelle G. Knight-Manuel and Joanne E. Marciano call culturally relevant education. But too rarely are these practices—those that centralize and build on the cultural strengths of students—cultivated and studied beyond a few teachers' respective classrooms. This book examines and showcases culturally relevant education in broader school contexts by learning from the voices of more than 500 teachers as well as other school leaders to consider what culturally relevant education means (and could look like) in an entire school space. The breadth and depth of this analysis cannot be overemphasized, as readers are able to build their knowledge about the role, salience, and importance of culturally relevant education. *Classroom Cultures: Equitable Schooling for Racially Diverse Youth* is a beautifully written book, provocatively showcasing what can happen when university professors endeavor to support local schools in their efforts to improve. A model for what other teacher education program faculty could do to support inservice teachers' development and learning, this book demonstrates important connections between theory and practice.

By co-constructing in-depth professional development opportunities across 28 schools in New York City serving more than 14,000 students, Knight-Manuel and Marciano are able to co-envision, co-construct, co-enact, and learn with teachers and school leaders. Their commitment to supporting practicing teachers is essential because, in Knight-Manuel and Marciano's words, "many preservice and inservice teachers who are deeply committed to their students have expressed concern about their preparation to implement a schoolwide approach to culturally relevant education . . . to teach their students, especially youth of Color." Readers of this work—especially those learning to teach in urban environments—have a powerful resource in this book. By systematically studying the words and practices of teachers, the authors show how curriculum and instruction can be designed to honor students' varied identity spaces and connect content with student interests.

In addition, Knight-Manuel and Marciano highlight the role and importance of educators' own self-learning, development, and assessment as they work to better meet the needs of their students. These authors learn from White teachers and teachers of Color. In other words, the authors demonstrate the importance of educators' identifying and naming their own privileges and the ways in which injustice and inequity work to maintain the status quo for White students and educators. Thus, the book tackles what I would describe as *the real and most difficult issues* of education today. The authors refuse to placate the White majority of teachers by pretending that the challenges in schools are a function of students. Rather, the authors make it clear that students succeed when mechanisms are in place to support them. It is our responsibility—educators in higher education and pre-K–12 learning contexts—to create spaces, practices, and systems to support students (all students!). Highlighting the ways in which White privilege and discrimination are common in schools and classrooms across the country, this book does not stop at outlining the problems. It offers real solutions for educators working hard to get better, and the practices identified can be transferred to other environments.

A refreshingly clear yet scholarly analysis, this book is a must-read for those of us in the fight for social justice. Grounded in theory and the established research, this work is a welcome addition to scholarship, written in ways that are accessible to real pre- and inservice practitioners—teachers, counselors, leaders, coaches, and social workers. Every teacher in teacher education—pre- and inservice—should read this book.

—H. Richard Milner IV
Cornelius Vanderbilt Professor of Education
author, *Rac(e)ing to Class*

Acknowledgments

We thank the New York City Department of Education and the ESI Team for welcoming us into this work. For their invaluable research assistance, we are grateful to Crystal Chen, Iesha Jackson, Errol Saunders, Denzil Streete, Kelly Zuckerman, Laura Vernikoff, Vaughn Watson, and Michael Wilson. We are also are deeply appreciative of Emily Spangler's encouragement and support in the development and writing of this book.

Michelle G. Knight-Manuel: I want to acknowledge the love, support, and encouragement of my loved ones, mentors, and friends. I thank my extraordinarily committed husband, Timothy Manuel, who literally drove me to and picked me up from many of the CRE-PD sessions throughout New York City, listened to my thoughts about the project, and encouraged me amid the many challenges to stay true to opening up opportunities with and for our youth. My mother has been with me on this journey over the years, and I have only the fondest memories of her coming to my conferences around the world, sitting and smiling with all the love and belief in her eldest daughter showing clearly in her eyes. My father is not far from my heart as I think about his desires for my life. Dad, we couldn't have imagined this journey if we tried. Over the years I've learned to appreciate and to be deeply thankful for my brothers, Richard, Michael, and Bill. Each brings his own unique strengths to our relationships and the well-being of our family. My sister Amy and niece Ava bring much joy and laughter into my life during their daily California car ride, as they give me advice and teach me how to play word games early in the morning. Much love to Reba and Maddy, who are so inspiring with their thirst for life, joy for adventures, and love for their grandmother. I wish only the best for Mychael as she starts her college journey. I hope that all of my nieces and nephews will continue to reach for the stars and may their dearest dreams come true. Finally, I give thanks for my mentors and friends. Ronald Rochon is an incredible mentor who has supported my personal goals, professional development, and scholarship since 1997. Knowing that Sylvia, Jessica, and Brontarina will be there to support at a moment's notice is a gift beyond compare. Finally, I offer this book in the spirit of hope—hope for a more equitable world—pressed down, shaken together, and running over.

Joanne E. Marciano: I am thankful for the opportunity to contribute to this work, particularly as it is made possible by the generosity of family, friends, colleagues, students, and young people with whom I continue to learn and grow. Vaughn, Carmela, and Carter, thank you for being the light that guides me on our collective journey. I love you with all that I am. To my family, Sam and Mary Marciano, Diana and Tony Brach, Tim and Alyssa Marciano, Laura Marciano-Sawh and Nick Sawh, Marion and Koach Coleman, Vance and Lori Watson, Victor and Adelia Watson, and my aunts, uncles, and cousins, I am thankful for your ever-present support and encouragement. I am also honored to serve as aunt and cousin to Joshua, Jarod, Jacob, Jon-Jon, Gabriel, Tehya, Tashawn, Kendall, Charlotte, Avery, Nick, Charlie, Dallas, Mateo, Brittne, Brianna, Brendan, Jaxon, Jace, Cooper, Vaughn, Aniyah, and Ava. Along with Carmela and Carter, you inspire me to envision and work toward a more just future. I am also thankful for the mentorship, love, and support of the late Paula Holmes, who created space for me to learn and grow alongside students and colleagues in ways that continue to profoundly impact my work and life.

CHAPTER 1

Introduction

We have our rose-colored glasses on because we teach here, we're under the impression that our boys are doing well. But then when we put them in the group with the Black and Latino [students from] the other schools and we see that they're not, and it pulls the glasses off of your face, you realize that we have to raise the expectations for them and their abilities. . . . I felt it [the professional development] encouraged us to be more attentive to them than we have been before. (Helena,* ESL teacher, White female, High School for Investigation and Inquiry, January–February 2013)

Honestly, I felt that I knew everything there could be, being a young man of Color growing up in New York City. Going to high school in New York City . . . I didn't know if there would be anything I could take away that would help me improve my instruction, as well as to improve how we deal with kids who are kind of in crisis and how we get them to be college and career ready. (Brandon, English teacher, Black male, Civic High School, 2013-2014)

Helena's and Brandon's statements give us a glimpse into their thoughts about their cultural identities as a White teacher and a teacher of Color, about the Black and Latinx** students they teach, and about their practices as secondary inservice teachers. They invite us to consider the importance of analyzing school data and their relationship to educational disparities experienced by students. Moreover, Helena and Brandon highlight the potential for professional development to support teachers in their commitments and practices as they pursue educational equity and social justice for all students, especially youth of Color. Interestingly, Helena and Brandon also reflect some of the established features of teachers who enact culturally relevant pedagogy as part of their classroom practices. Culturally relevant pedagogy is a comprehensive framework, rooted in equity, that addresses teaching and learning opportunity

---

* All names of people and schools in the book are pseudonyms except the authors' names, Michelle and Joanne.

** In seeking to be gender inclusive, we use the term Latinx when referring to peoples of Latin American descent, except when referring specifically to groups of people or individuals identified by gender, such as Latino young men or Latina young women (Monzo, 2016).

1

gaps by building from students' cultural backgrounds, interests, and experiences as strengths in learning and creating new knowledge (Ladson-Billings, 1994, 2009). In learning to enact a culturally relevant pedagogical approach in their own practices, Helena and Brandon adopted a learner lens; expressed a willingness to engage in critical self-examination, including "introspection that brings to the fore their own strengths, weaknesses, privileges, and issues"; and sought to develop high expectations for their students (Milner, 2017, p. 24). Enacting culturally relevant teaching and learning practices throughout a school environment can provide more-equitable opportunities to ensure that all students, particularly culturally and linguistically diverse students, are supported academically, socially, emotionally, and civically in an increasingly diverse, global society. In the midst of pressing societal and educational disparities, however, many preservice and inservice teachers who are deeply committed to their students have expressed concern about their preparation to implement a schoolwide approach to culturally relevant education (CRE) to teach their students, especially youth of Color. We are in agreement with such researchers as Ladson-Billings (1994) and Milner (2017) that all teachers can be prepared to work successfully with all students.

In this book, *Classroom Cultures: Equitable Schooling for Racially Diverse Youth*, we focus on the perspectives and practices of more than 500 teachers and school leaders from 28 school communities who participated in a series of professional development workshops we designed and facilitated across 2½ years. We examine educators' experiences in culturally relevant education professional development (CRE-PD) to better understand how to support educators in creating equitable schooling environments for increasingly culturally, ethnically, and linguistically diverse students in our nation's schools, particularly Black and Latino young men (see Appendix A). We sought to address the following questions: How do teachers and school leaders make sense of culturally relevant education? What influence do culturally relevant education professional development workshops have on their beliefs, knowledge, and practices? Specifically, we highlight the complexities and challenges teachers and school leaders experienced as they developed their capacity to provide culturally relevant teaching and learning opportunities for students of Color in their classrooms and schools. We also offer recommendations about the implementation of a schoolwide approach to CRE to support students of Color. In so doing, we provide direct insight into practical strategies for creating and sustaining a culturally relevant schoolwide approach that positions school communities as sites of critical inquiry to create more-equitable learning opportunities for students.

This chapter explores what culturally relevant education is, why it is necessary, and the need for CRE-PD in order to support teachers in teaching all students, especially their students of Color. As you continue to read about the current educational and social context in which we live, we invite you to critically reflect on your role as an educator and/or school leader within this context and how professional development might support your commitments to educating all youth to their highest potential.

WHY IS CHANGE NECESSARY?

Given the educational and social climate, four factors have converged to create an urgent need for a national teaching force that is well prepared to address issues of race, equity, and pedagogy as they teach all students, particularly youth of Color. First, teachers and students in the United States are grappling with ongoing racial turmoil between police and communities of Color (Blad, 2015; Camera, 2015; Jernigan & Daniel, 2011) and current political rhetoric laced with tensions around race, immigration, and religion (Costello, 2016). Second, shifting migration patterns across cities and suburbs have created "de facto diverse communities" (Wells, Fox, & Cordova-Cobo, 2016, p. 3). For example, 41% of students educated in suburban school districts are non-White, an increase from 28% in the early 1990s (Fry, 2009). Simultaneously, White families are moving back to cities as they have become more attractive cultural centers (Wells et al., 2016). Third, global migration has contributed to changing demographics within states and cities nationwide. For instance, over the past 10 years, immigrant communities have been growing in smaller cities like Dayton, Ohio, and Indianapolis, Indiana, and rural areas of North Carolina, places not always thought of as immigrant settlement destinations (Maciag, 2016). In addition to the demographic shifts, teachers and students are experiencing angry and xenophobic rhetoric around immigrant communities, which has risen dramatically in recent years (Costello, 2016). Fourth, the K–12 population in 2013 grew to 50% students of Color, with more than 54% of the K–12 population expected to be students of Color by the year 2025 (National Center for Education Statistics, 2018b).

Yet, even as schools nationwide comprise an increasingly diverse study body, disproportionate educational outcomes continue to impact the lives and success of students of Color, first-generation college applicants, and students from low-income neighborhoods (U.S. Department of Education Office for Civil Rights, 2016). An urgent need exists to examine and address persistent inequities that negatively impact educational opportunities experienced by youth of Color across urban, suburban, and rural school contexts. For example, the National Center for Education Statistics (2018c) indicates that 76% of Black students and 79% of Latinx students graduated from high school in 2015–16 as compared with 88% of White students and 91% of Asian students. Moreover, Black and Latino young men continue to enroll in college at rates much lower than those of White young men, and disproportionately attend 2-year colleges. For example, in 2016, 40% of White 18- to 24-year-old males were in enrolled in college, while 33%

of Black 18- to 24-year-old males and 35% of Hispanic 18- to 24-year-old young men were enrolled in college (National Center for Education Statistics, 2018a). Data for the percentages of Asian young men enrolled in college were not provided by the National Center for Education Statistics (2018a). At the root of the disparities surrounding high school completion and college-readiness data is the reality that many Black and Latinx students encounter markedly inadequate educational opportunities, such as fewer curricular and co-curricular offerings in high school (Eskenazi, Eddins, & Beam, 2003; Knight & Marciano, 2013). In addition, teachers' expectations for, beliefs about, and dispositions toward students impact their outcomes, with students of Color and students living in poverty facing lower expectations and inequitable access to high-quality learning opportunities (Conklin, Hawley, Powell, & Ritter, 2010). Therefore, even as the curricular and pedagogical practices we share throughout this book may create productive learning opportunities for all students, we explicitly focus our attention on how educators may recognize, challenge, and change inequitable schooling experiences too often encountered by Black and Latinx youth.

Improving the educational experiences of students enrolled in schools across the country as a means to support their access to postsecondary education and future careers is of national concern. School district leaders, superintendents, and principals increasingly are seeking to provide professional development for teachers to learn how they can create and implement equity-minded, school-based reforms such as a schoolwide approach to culturally relevant education to support all students. Recently, for example, the mayor of New York City announced a $23 million investment in the next 4 years for culturally responsive practices and anti-bias professional development for all New York City Department of Education staff members before the completion of the 2021–22 academic year (Chapman, 2018). The need for equipping educators and school leaders with the knowledge, skills, and dispositions to teach using a comprehensive culturally relevant pedagogical approach is greater now than ever.

WHAT IS CULTURALLY RELEVANT EDUCATION?

Culturally relevant education is a conceptual framework that recognizes the importance of including students' cultural backgrounds, interests, and lived experiences in all aspects of teaching and learning within the classroom and across the school (Ladson-Billings, 1994, 2009; Milner, 2017). Culturally relevant education is viewed as critical in improving student engagement and achievement, and college readiness and success for all youth, particularly for youth of Color. Specifically, CRE is a comprehensive teaching approach that empowers all students intellectually, socially, emotionally, and politically by using cultural referents to impact knowledge, skills, and attitudes (Ladson-Billings, 1994, 2009). We purposefully take up the three interconnected tenets of CRE identified by Gloria Ladson Billings that emerged from understanding the practices of successful Black and White teachers of African American students. These tenets include an emphasis on (1) student learning and achievement, (2) the affirmation of students' cultural competence, and (3) the facilitation of a sociopolitical/critical consciousness that facilitates students' understandings and critique of inequities within educational and social institutions.

Student Learning and Achievement

Student learning opportunities reflect teachers' expectations, beliefs, values, and norms of learning within classrooms and across schools (e.g., curriculum, standards, and extracurricular activities). Culturally relevant teachers clearly explain what achievement means in their classrooms and how students can obtain it through a variety of measures, especially as they believe all students are capable of learning, achieving academic success, and being prepared for college and careers after high school. In addition, culturally relevant educators understand the importance of making explicit their high expectations for the academic achievement of all students, and demystifying the processes of enrolling in college and pursuing careers. For example, one high school we collaborated with was recognized by the New York City Department of Education for a particularly promising practice: In order to better prepare their students, 90% of whom were Black and Latinx, to compete for college admissions and jobs in STEM fields, the educators chose to increase the academic rigor of their programs by adding computer science classes and opportunities for youth to learn from the real-world experiences of volunteer industry professionals.

Cultural Competence

Student learning opportunities reflecting cultural competence build on the cultural knowledge and experiences that youth and their families bring to school. Culturally relevant teachers affirm students' cultural backgrounds as assets, building on knowledge students possess to assist them in learning new concepts, while supporting their academic and college-going identities. For instance, an administrator at the High School for Investigation and Inquiry noted that the Danielson framework used for evaluating teacher performance across schools in New York City created opportunities for teachers to be recognized for including culturally relevant curriculum in their classes. The sharing of personal experiences of bigotry and bias by teachers and students before a lesson about *Brown v. Board of Education* could be considered an example of culturally relevant curriculum. Another school, Founders High School, was recognized by the New York City Department of Education for their partnerships with community-based organizations and other community stakeholders. A fraternal organization of African American professional males answered the call, and together they created a civil service career pathways program to create a school environment that promoted excellence, leadership, and personal responsibility.

Critical Consciousness/Sociopolitical Awareness

Student learning opportunities that foreground the development of critical consciousness and sociopolitical awareness are linked to understandings and critiques of educational and societal inequities. Culturally relevant teachers support the sociopolitical consciousness of their students, so that students are able to develop a critical stance toward inequities in their schools, in their communities, and within the larger society. For example, a principal we collaborated with at Civic High School discussed the purpose of a 1-day retreat for Black males that the school offered, which included an examination of the Black Lives Matter movement. Specifically, students were guided in considering obstacles they might encounter to their academic and social development due to their appearance, language, and physical movements. One educator at City Leadership Academy was concerned about having a discussion on wearing hoodies, especially in light of Trayvon Martin's death. She shared, "We need to tell them the truth. We need to teach them how they are perceived and the need for them to code-switch. [We need to] talk about wearing a hoody in certain environments" (5/29/2014). Youth also discussed their experiences with and considerations of police brutality, racism, identity, and self-worth, highlighting their outrage and anxiety over the untimely deaths of Black men, including Eric Garner and Michael Brown, and the countless silenced Black women and girls, including Sandra Bland, Alberta Spruill, and Shelley Frey, at the hands of police throughout the United States.

These three tenets of culturally relevant teaching are crucial in supporting students' productive daily interactions with teachers and peers, providing a rigorous and relevant curriculum, and promoting the development of youth as socially conscious and civic-minded individuals. Research has shown these tenets may be enacted by teachers of Color and White educators. For example, Milner (2017) argues that an essential finding of Gloria Ladson-Billings's (2009) research on culturally relevant education is that "teachers from any racial and ethnic background could be successful with any racial group of students when they possessed or developed the knowledge, attitudes, dispositions, beliefs, skills and practices necessary to meet students' needs" (p. 2). As teachers who previously taught middle and high school students and currently teach pre- and inservice teachers, our work with teachers and school leaders across the CRE-PD was based on this belief.

In addition to the three tenets of culturally relevant pedagogy defined by Gloria Ladson Billings, our work also is informed by emerging educational research highlighting the importance of creating and developing cultural-ly sustaining educational opportunities for youth navigating inequitable schooling experiences (Paris, 2012; Paris & Alim, 2014, 2017). We use primarily the term and stances of culturally relevant education through-out this book, as this is the stance that the New York City Department of Education asked us to use in our work with educators in the CRE-PD and was the term participants were most familiar with. However, we recognize the importance of considering culturally sustaining pedagogies as drawing attention to the multiple global, cultural, and linguistic identities continuing to emerge from today's youth culture, including art, literature, music, ath-letics, and film (Ladson-Billings, 2014; Paris & Alim, 2017). We therefore build from recent work on culturally sustaining pedagogies throughout this book, as appropriate, to further understandings of how such pedagogies may be incorporated into educators' practices in addition to culturally rele-vant practices more explicitly discussed.

MOVING TO SHARED UNDERSTANDINGS OF CRE AND CULTURE

When we asked educators across several schools, during our first session together, to write a brief response to explain what they knew about cul-turally responsive education, we learned two very important lessons. First, it became evident that educators, even those working in the same schools, had different understandings of what CRE is. We realized that while some of the educators focused on notions of student learning and achievement in a general, broad sense, we rarely heard educators discuss how CRE also promotes affirming and sustaining students' cultural identities or provides avenues for critiquing the injustices students were experiencing or witness-ing in society. Second, supporting educators in developing considerations of varied notions of culture became extremely important in understanding the dynamic, evolving nature of culture in people's lives. For example, we found that educators' initial considerations of culture included notions that culture was unchanging or applied to entire groups of people. In addition, educators often had not considered how individuals participate as members of multiple cultural groups and have varied experiences within and across those groups.

As we moved to shared understandings of culturally relevant educa-tion and more-nuanced considerations of culture, educators expressed a willingness to re-examine their ideas and envision what CRE could look like in schools and classrooms. For example, during our very first CRE-PD session in 2013, we asked teachers, administrators, and school support staff to write down what they already knew about CRE. Some participants left the response completely blank, while others wrote, "not very much," and, "the very basics," respectively. One educator noted that she knew of it only superficially and that the objective of being culturally responsive was to meet the needs of young people of Color; another shared a more advanced understanding, noting that CRE "reflects and embodies the culture of students you are servicing. It should also focus on the positive aspects of the culture and validate the 'misunderstood or misinterpreted' aspects." Additional ideas raised included one participant's consideration that CRE means "using students' prior knowledge and experiences to build on their academics." Educators further noted CRE's focus on identity, with one writing, "CRE starts with identity. Then looking at the context of that identity, most importantly, teachers have to have an understanding of the various identities within our school." A personal connection was made by another participant who noted, "I was raised in NYC of immigrant parents and I believe I had to navigate these same waters as my students." Connections to students' experiences outside of school were further emphasized by an educator who noted how CRE "is about looking beyond the classroom."

In addressing these varied understandings, one of our first goals in the CRE-PD was to develop common, shared understanding of culturally relevant pedagogy using Gloria Ladson-Billings's three tenets of culturally relevant teaching: student learning and achievement, cultural competence, and sociopolitical awareness/critical consciousness. We engaged educators in looking at their own practices through culturally relevant indicators that they could return to again and again throughout the CRE-PD sessions (see Appendix B). We then sought to get into deeper considerations and shared understandings of culture to answer educators' questions, including:

- What does culture mean in *culturally relevant*?
- Whose culture are we talking about when we say *culturally relevant pedagogies*?

UNDERSTANDING CULTURE IN CULTURALLY RELEVANT EDUCATION

I really enjoyed the multiple definitions of culture. The knowledge to include multiple perspectives of a culture. It was valuable to see how my colleagues view race and culture. Culture is interpreted differently based on your environment and your family values. (City Leadership Academy, Anonymous evaluative teacher feedback, 2015)

This educator's evaluative feedback acknowledged that the conversation and activities on notions of culture were one of the teacher's "aha" moments of the day. Our sustained engagement with educators participating in the CRE-PD over time also provided further opportunities to facilitate deeper understandings of culture and what it meant for their practices. In general, notions of race and ethnicity often are conflated with notions of culture (Milner, 2017). Moreover, static notions of culture tend to essentialize different populations, especially Black and Latino young men. By essentialize, we mean to see all students within a group as the same, rather than recognizing the heterogeneity and different lived experiences that many youth of Color experience based on, for example, language, immigrant status, and/or gender, in addition to race/ethnicity. Thus, "culture is not only about race; race is a central aspect of culture, and for some racial and ethnic groups, race is the most salient feature of their cultural identity" (Milner, 2017, p. 5; see also Milner, 2015). Popular culture, such as television, movies, and music, moves educators to consider "a hybridity, fluidity, and complexity [of student identities] never before considered in schools and classrooms" (Ladson-Billings, 2014, p. 82; see also Paris & Alim, 2017). To support educators in developing shared understandings of culture and its connection to culturally relevant pedagogies, we took time to better understand what educators and school leaders meant by the word *culture* and whether they were conflating it with race. In so doing, we hoped to work against static notions of culture and essentialist views of youth of Color, which, in turn, influence how educators take up CRE in their practices.

We found that one way to begin conversations with educators about how they might challenge singular understandings of culture emerged from their engagement with popular culture. For example, educators at one particular school met for weekly CRE-PD sessions on Thursday afternoons, the day after new episodes of the television program *Empire* typically aired. Teachers often arrived at the PD sessions eager to discuss the previous night's episode. Michelle joined these informal conversations about the show, making connections between educators' lived experiences watching the television program and their engagement in the CRE-PD. For example, Michelle invited educators to consider how the storylines featured on *Empire* reflected notions of Black culture. She then encouraged the educators to discuss whether and how their own lived experiences and the experiences of youth of Color with whom they worked were reflected (or not) across the television program.

In building from their interest in the television program, Michelle guided educators in understanding, as Geneva Gay (2010) asserts, that culture is central, but also multidimensional, dynamic, multifaceted, and influenced by (and influencing) a variety of factors. Similarly, Milner (2017) notes that "culture can be defined as deep-rooted values, beliefs, languages, customs, and norms shared among a group of people. . . . Culture is a dynamic concept that encompasses, among other areas, racial and ethnic identity, class, language, economic status, and gender" (p. 5). We further challenged educators to reconsider deficit perspectives of culture that position students and families as solely responsible for their failures, without any consideration given to the societal structural inequities they may face. Instead, we supported educators in considering research focused on the assets and strengths of a community to support the academic success of children and youth in schools (Miller Dyce & Owusu-Ansah, 2016; Moll, Amanti, Neff, & Gonzalez, 2005; Yosso, 2005). Throughout this book, we often return to this understanding of culture as dynamic and fluid to undergird the ways in which educators took up varied topics, such as fostering productive teacher–student relationships through a culturally relevant lens.

RESEARCH STUDY

The research study examining the CRE-PD and discussed throughout the book is situated within public schools in New York City (see Appendix C for more information). In August 2011, the New York City mayor, New York City schools chancellor, and George Soros of the Open Society Foundation announced the Expanded Success Initiative (ESI) as a component of New York City's Young Men's Initiative, to change the lives of children and youth attending school in New York City (esinyc.com/about/). ESI was designed specifically to counter the challenge that the 4-year high school graduation rate in 2010 for Black and Latino young men was 52% and 54% respectively. Of those who graduated, only 18% and 21% respectively were considered college and career ready (Expanded Success Initiative, 2012). The 5-year, $24 million investment supported initiatives focused on education.

A major focus of ESI's implementation was the introduction of culturally relevant education professional development in Fall 2012 to build institutional capacity among teachers and school leaders to support the educational experiences and college readiness of Black and Latino young men. This commitment was reflected through CRE-PD opportunities for educators across 40 high schools, with the purpose of creating more-equitable learning opportunities in the daily educational experiences of Black and Latino young men and preparing them to be college and career ready. Fewer than 10 of the 40 high schools focused their mission explicitly on career readiness (Villavicencio, Klevan, & Kemple, 2018). ESI developed professional learning communities of practice focused on the achievement of Black and Latino young men, with the intent to scale successful culturally relevant practices and college access strategies citywide in schools serving more than 1 million children.

All of the schools participating in ESI met the following criteria: (1) at least 35% of enrollment was Black and Latino males; (2) at least 60% of enrolled students qualified for free and/or reduced lunch; and (3) the school graduated at least 65% of its students in 4 years. Although schools had 4-year graduation rates higher than the city's average, the schools eligible for inclusion had a substantially lower score, less than 12.5%, on a college readiness index (CRI). The CRI includes the percentage of students demonstrating a level of proficiency in reading, writing, and mathematics that allows them to avoid remedial coursework at local colleges.

We provided in-depth professional development with teachers and school leaders across 28 ESI schools. The school leaders volunteered their schools to participate in the CRE-PD we offered. Teachers across the majority of participating schools reflect demographics similar to those in many of the nation's schools, where more than 70% of the teaching force is White, female, and middle class (Urban Institute, 2017). In many studies, researchers also have noted that very little of the experiences, identities, and prior knowledge of teachers of Color is taken into account in teacher preparation and professional development (Jackson & Knight-Manuel, 2018; Kohli & Pizarro, 2016; Lipman, 1996). Our work in this book focuses on how both White teachers and teachers of Color made sense of and enacted culturally relevant pedagogical practices. The 28 schools served more than 14,000 students, who attended large comprehensive schools with over 1,000 students, small schools with 300–600 students, two schools that focused on career and technical education, and 26 schools that focused on college preparation (Harper & Associates, 2014).

While the schools represented in the CRE-PD varied in size and focus as described above, our analysis of educators' experiences demonstrated that the visible support and presence of school leaders in the CRE-PD played a significant role in how teachers across these varied school contexts took up the culturally relevant education practices in their own work. For example, teachers told us they appreciated school leaders who also participated in asking questions, making themselves vulnerable to addressing the inequities within their schools. Teachers also shared how the involvement of school administrators in the CRE-PD impacted how they thought about the role of CRE in teacher evaluations, such as the Danielson framework utilized in New York City public schools. Moreover, in 24 of the 28 schools, teachers volunteered to participate in the CRE-PD, whereas it was mandated in six of the schools. Teachers also noted that the CRE-PD had more of an impact in schools where it was a schoolwide effort. In one school, Metropolitan High School, where the CRE-PD was not mandated for everyone, the teachers turnkeyed the ideas with their colleagues.

We center the perspectives of the educators and school leaders who participated in inquiry-oriented CRE-PD to support the daily educational experiences, identities, and college readiness of Black (e.g., African American, African, Caribbean) and Latino males (e.g., Dominican, Puerto Rican, Mexican). Many of these young men were also first-generation college applicants from low-income neighborhoods. Even though the CRE-PD focused on improving educational opportunities for Black and Latino young men, we recognize the importance of challenging inequitable schooling opportunities for young women as well. We therefore highlight additional opportunities to support more-equitable schooling experiences for culturally, ethnically, and linguistically diverse young men and women. Such opportunities further consider the New York City Department of Education's interest in scaling up practices shared in the CRE-PD with educators throughout the city, not only for Black and Latino young men.

We specifically chose to design and facilitate inquiry-oriented professional learning because such approaches have been deemed effective in uniquely providing educators space to collaborate with one another, actively participate in learning activities, engage with particular problems of practice, and self-evaluate as they seek to examine and modify their practices to address educational inequities that affect students of Color (Devereaux, Prater, Jackson, Heath, & Carter, 2010; Pollock, Bocala, Deckman, & Dickstein-Staub, 2016). The teachers' and school leaders' perspectives inform how schools can build teachers' capacity to better understand what culturally relevant education is, what it looks like in practice, and how to enact it in their own practices. As you read, we invite you to consider how implementing culturally relevant education as an equity-minded reform can affect the academic and social achievement of all children, especially African American and Latinx youth in your school.

OVERVIEW OF THE CONTENTS—
CRE: WHAT DOES IT LOOK LIKE IN PRACTICE?

This book is organized into seven chapters. Our explicit goal is to support the capacity of teachers and school leaders to create more-equitable learning environments for all youth, particularly culturally and linguistically diverse youth. Each of Chapters 2–6 begins with an inquiry-oriented question and opportunity that connect to the topic of the chapter. We provide multiple examples of how educators take up ideas of race, equity, and pedagogy to support the academic, emotional, social, and civic educational opportunities for Black and Latino young men. We interweave connections to the educational research literature, highlighting particular themes about teaching and learning and the ways that educators may interact with culturally diverse youth to support their educational experiences, postsecondary pathways, and life outcomes. In the sections of each chapter titled "Everyday Practices in Context" and "Autobiographical Reflection," we share our own experiences utilizing a culturally relevant approach when working in middle/secondary schools as well with preservice and inservice teachers. The chapters conclude with what CRE looks like in practice in three areas: (1) curriculum and instruction, (2) school culture, and (3) college readiness and access. Chapter 7, the concluding chapter, synthesizes our main arguments and implications for schools serving culturally, racially, and linguistically diverse youth, and seeking to provide professional development within a schoolwide approach to CRE.

**QUESTIONS AND ACTIONS FOR INDIVIDUALS AND
SMALL GROUPS WITHIN SCHOOL COMMUNITIES**

1. As you reflect on some of the responses about what CRE is and how educators are thinking about notions of culture in this chapter, whom do you identify with and how might you define or understand culturally relevant education?
2. Which of the three tenets of Gloria Ladson-Billings's framework on CRE do you feel most confident in implementing in your own work with students?
3. Which areas would you like further support in as part of the process of becoming a more culturally relevant educator?
4. Gather and examine data on the performance of one specific population of students enrolled in your school (e.g., Black and Latino young men, English language learners, students in special education, girls in science). Think about these data and how the ensuing chapters can assist in creating more-equitable schooling for this population.

CHAPTER 2

Understanding Teachers' Racial Identities, Experiences, and Culturally Relevant Pedagogical Practices

Inquiry Focus: How does reflecting on race, identities, inequities, and culturally relevant practices support educators in creating learning opportunities for youth of Color?

Opportunity: Educators who have a better understanding of their own identities are better positioned to understand and teach all students, especially students of Color.

Lillian: "It's important you have your own definition of self. We need to teach our children that they should not be defined. They need to define themselves."

Sara: "How do we do that?"

Lillian: "We have to know ourselves first because you can't teach something you don't know." (Observation notes, Metropolitan High School, 12/3/2013)

Yes, and that came out in some of the PD [sessions] about how some of the teachers were saying that maybe because they had White privilege, they may not be able to relate to someone growing up in a Section 8 housing . . . or single-family households and they [the teachers] have both parents . . . yeah I think there was some anxiety with that. Now whether there is the training they can do to help lower that anxiety, I don't know. I think that some people do have that anxiety here. (Interview, Civic High School, 4/8/2014)

In the exchanges above, Lillian and Sara make visible some of the tensions that emerge as educators seek to enact culturally relevant practices that support the educational experiences of the culturally, ethnically, and linguistically diverse youth they teach. Lillian's assertion, for example, that students "need to define themselves" appears to take up an asset-oriented approach to supporting youth naming and affirming their own identities rather than having others define who they are or can be. Teaching youth of Color to "define themselves" assumes that they are the central figures involved in this work, an assumption the current political and cultural context in the United States does not allow us to fully make. Youth of Color continue to confront deficit-oriented stereotypes in the media, as well as through popular culture, about who they are and what they can achieve in life. We argue that before educators can support all students, it is critical that they understand their own racial, ethnic, and linguistic identities (Colomer, 2018; Howard, 2003) and how they might recognize their own biases and benefits from privilege. A single monolithic experience of any cultural group does not exist (Colomer, 2018). With such understandings, for example, teachers are better equipped to talk with their colleagues and students about their racial, ethnic, and linguistic identities and experiences. Given the similarities and differences of race, ethnicity, and/or linguistic identities between and among teachers and students, these understandings also could affirm and sustain students' racial, ethnic, linguistic, and academic identities to support youth throughout their educational experiences.

Equally important, as revealed in Lillian's second statement above, is that notions of White privilege are acknowledged and located in personal experiences, while at the same time allowing for evasion and distancing of educators from systemic structural racial injustices that create vast disparities in wealth, education, and housing. Leonardo (2004) argues that "the discourse on privilege comes with the psychological effect of personalizing racism rather than understanding its structural origins in interracial relations" (p. 140). For example, some people may personally feel that they did not participate in slavery in the United States (Vaught & Castagno, 2008) and therefore they do not recognize the continued systems of oppression encountered by Black people today. This limited perspective can show itself in a lack of understanding and bias toward people of Color and groups, like Black Lives Matter or the #MeToo movement, that work to dismantle systems of oppression of race and gender. Implied in the statement of the educator who named the intersection of White privilege and the teaching of students in Section 8 housing are the questions: What does it mean to be White and middle class in society, and how do these identities impact educators' pedagogical practices, especially with students of Color? We argue that all educators need professional learning opportunities to explore and critically reflect on their multiple social identity markers, such as class, gender, language, ability, sexual orientation, and notions of privilege, in order to build the capacity to better relate and connect to their colleagues and students with varied personal and family histories (Kozleski, 2010).

In this chapter, we highlight understandings and challenges that emerged for teachers as they explored their own racial/ethnic, linguistic, and cultural identities, and the identities of their colleagues, which might or might not be similar to those of their students. We invite educators to take up the following question: How can understanding my own racial, ethnic, and cultural identities help me to better understand my students in order to create more culturally relevant and sustaining pedagogies in my class and the school? Moreover, in what ways can educators be supported in exploring their understandings of their multiple identities? Culturally relevant educators see themselves in community with others. We contend that teachers and school leaders can begin to enter into conversations with one another and critically reflect about race, culture, their own cultural identities, inequities within schools and society, and how students are being impacted by these inequities. As Durden, Dooley, and Truscott (2014) note, "Regardless of his or her racial or cultural origin, [a culturally relevant teacher has] a conscious understanding of systemic inequities and structures that impact the success and opportunities of racially diverse students" (p. 1004). Similarly, during one of the district meetings of ESI Liaisons, teachers and school leaders from all 40 schools participating in the ESI initiative, Robert, a teacher from Metropolitan High School, remarked:

> The one [principle] that is often left out of the classroom is social–political consciousness, education does not exist in a vacuum . . . we often forget that they have lives and things that affected them. I went to an all-boys Catholic school. I was the first to get there and the last to leave. People thought that it was because I was such a good student, but it was because I lived in a neighborhood that was dangerous and individuals with uniforms would get jumped. [. . .] If you see someone fall asleep, it may be that they live in a shelter or were working. You shouldn't always take things personally, sometimes it is just their reaction to things outside of school. (Observation notes, 11/17/2013)

Robert's comments open up the idea that culturally relevant classrooms must take into account the context in which the students are living and how that impacts their relationships and behavior in school, which, in turn, influences teachers' pedagogical practices. Camangian (2010) argues that "leaving urban youth relationships to heal on their own—without deliberately addressing them in our classrooms—shows a lack of responsibility and little regard for how we respond to human relationships confronting students of Color in their communities" (p. 180). Or as Marc, another teacher, noted, "I work with young people outside of school and think they are brilliant, then find out that they are failing all their classes. You might see their competence outside of the classroom but see them silent in your classroom. So that's a bridge [for teachers to build upon]" (observation notes, 2/14/2013). Culturally relevant educators are able to connect to school and home cultures to support learning opportunities. The goals of the CRE-PD included supporting the capacity of teachers to better understand their own racial and cultural identities in order to develop optimal learning environments for their students, particularly their Black and Latino male students.

Therefore, we highlight examples of how educators' participation in the CRE-PD gave them time and space to have conversations with colleagues and critically reflect about their race, culture, and inequities related to different identities. Not surprisingly, for many of the educators this focus initially was uncomfortable given that they had never before been provided with a space to develop a sense of their own racial/ethnic identities within the school context. White educators, in particular, across multiple schools attested to the fact that they had been teaching for many years and never had a conversation about race with their colleagues at school. As one teacher shared, "Being at a table with people, like my own co-workers, but them being different races too . . . kind of being okay with talking about certain things that usually you don't talk about" (3/31/2014). Another educator noted:

> I'm a White Jewish male, and we talk a lot about it in the history class, cultural diffusion, where we see it, how we can bring it in. . . . When I first started teaching here 18 years ago I didn't know what I was stepping into. I felt like I was a world away. So, not only breaking up [into small groups] with other teachers and hearing their backgrounds, but seeing that we *share* a lot of commonalities in our classrooms always helps me. (Josh, Interview, High School for Investigation and Inquiry, 4/2014)

While several teachers of Color noted that they had many opportunities to reflect on their racial and ethnic identities in other contexts such as within their family, they too need opportunities to reflect on how their racial and cultural identities impact their pedagogical practices (Colomer, 2018; Jackson & Knight-Manuel, 2018). Researchers argue that it is exactly this type of personal and group reflection that can serve as a prelude to creating culturally relevant teaching strategies (Milner, 2003, 2012). For example, educators who are not comfortable talking about issues of race may ignore or remain unaware of the racial biases students of Color encounter across their daily lived experiences. Therefore, reflections about race, culture, and privilege support both White teachers and teachers of Color in their capacity to teach the whole student—academically, socially, emotionally, and politically. As educators engage with one another around the fluidity of identities and the varied, heterogeneous nature of cultural groups, they open up opportunities to understand how race and other social identity markers influence their own culturally relevant and sustaining practices with students.

Often, as teacher educators, we have heard the question, "Where do I begin to think about race?" In other instances, we heard from secondary teachers, "Why do I need to do this? I just teach kids," thereby taking a color-blind pedagogical approach. To address educators who might be ready to begin critical reflections about race as well as about the tensions surrounding notions of color blindness and color consciousness, we laid the groundwork to support teachers in developing the skills and knowledge to talk about their racial/ethnic identities and those of their students. Racial color blindness generally is posed as a positive idea that overlooking or ignoring racial and ethnic differences promotes racial harmony and that race has no consequences for "a person's status and well-being" (Rosenberg, 2004, p. 257). Therefore, there is no recognition of the harm in a color-blind racial ideology that occurs in interpersonal interactions, institutional polices/practices (Annamma, Jackson, & Morrison, 2017; Neville, Gallardo, & Sue, 2016; Ullucci & Battey, 2011), and the ensuing disparities and inequities, for instance, in education, wealth, housing, health care, justice, and employment. A color-blind racial stance enables some teachers to avoid the realization that while they may deny their own racial/ethnic identity, their students, in many cases, interact with them as racialized beings (Valli, 1995).

By color consciousness, we mean the ways in which teachers are aware of race and the role it plays in students' lives and the opportunity gaps experienced by students of color. Culturally relevant teachers reject color-blind racial ideologies and pedagogies that do not acknowledge race as a central dimension of teachers' and students' identities, lives, and experiences (Milner, 2017; Valli, 1995). Rejecting color-blind racial ideologies creates opportunities for educators to examine their own racial identities, to be mindful of the disparities in achievement among different racial/ethnic groups, and to engage the ways in which students' cultural backgrounds, interests, and identities are drawn upon as strengths in curriculum. For educators to enact teaching and curriculum that are inclusive of diverse students' histories, cultures, and knowledges, they must be aware of those histories, cultures, and knowledges rather than assume color-blind approaches that privilege White middle-class norms. Moreover, educators must consider how students of Color see and interact with teachers as racialized human beings. A color-conscious approach would not evade, but rather address, the anxiety that the teacher at the beginning of this chapter expressed in teaching students from Section 8 housing.

We sought to support teachers' capacities to critically reflect on race in their cultural contexts through discussions of race in everyday practice and through two pedagogical inquiry activities. Taken together, these approaches created opportunities for educators to better understand their own cultural identities and to reflect about "themselves in relation to others' racial identities, issues and experiences, and reject commonly held beliefs and stereotypes" (Milner, 2003, p. 176). Sharing their identities within specific cultural contexts also gives educators the potential to humanize one another as they learn about the similarities and differences in their own and their students' experiences in educational and societal contexts (Camangian, 2010). Specifically, we share the nuanced ways participants negotiated tensions related to perceptions of their racial and cultural identities. Then in Chapter 3 we turn our attention to the influence the understandings of their identities and these negotiations had on their teaching practices with youth of Color, their families, and their communities.

EVERYDAY PRACTICES IN CONTEXT

As a White, female teacher working in a school serving predominantly Black and, increasingly, Latinx students and their families, Joanne initially did not realize how important it was to be in conversation with students about stereotypes they might have of her as a White person. However, multiple experiences across her career as an educator taught her otherwise. Students held stereotypes about her as a White woman, and also when they learned she was Italian.

For example, during one class early in the school year, students asked Joanne if she was Jewish. She is not, and when she asked students why they thought she might be, they shared that she sometimes wore a long black skirt to school and had dark brown hair. Joanne was confused about their reasoning and asked the students to clarify. Students shared that there were many Jewish women in the nearby neighborhoods of Williamsburg and Crown Heights, Brooklyn, who dressed in long black skirts and had dark brown hair. Joanne later came to understand some of the tensions that had arisen between the Black and Jewish communities, particularly in Crown Heights (Goldschmidt, 2006), and realized that students were bringing their own experiences with racial and ethnic relationships into their encounters with her, even as she remained unaware of the sociohistorical context of the community near the school and students' relationships to it.

When Joanne, as part of that same conversation, told students she was Italian, a student named Arnold stood up from his seat near the back of the classroom, shouted a line from one of the *Godfather* movies, and made a gesture reflective of the violence represented in the film. Joanne pushed past her initial feelings of discomfort and asked Arnold to take his seat. He did, and when she explained that she found stereotypes about being affiliated with the Italian mafia offensive, Arnold apologized. Another student, Hector, then asked Joanne if she ate only spaghetti and meatballs. Again, Joanne was discomforted that students she had worked with for several weeks by that time would not only hold, but voice, stereotypes about her based on her Italian background. But the relationships Joanne had established with students led her to push back against Hector's comment as well. Joanne asked whether Hector really thought it was possible she would eat only spaghetti and meatballs for her entire life. Hadn't he actually been inside her classroom during lunch and classroom celebrations and seen her eat other things? In reflecting on the conversation, Joanne realized that many of the other students also might have held those stereotypes about her, but it was Arnold and Hector who felt comfortable enough to directly address them with her. The realization led Joanne to more explicitly share her racial and ethnic background with students early in the school year as she positioned herself as a learner alongside students. For example, Joanne shared her expectation that they would each draw upon their cultural backgrounds and lived experiences as they collaborated across the course of the academic year.

Throughout the CRE-PD, teachers mentioned they became very aware that students might be stereotyping them also and that they did not feel comfortable addressing these stereotypes, especially as they had not had any preparation in reflecting on their own cultural identities in their school context. Being comfortable with one's own identities and stereotypes affords opportunities for teachers to share with their students the realities of their own lives while also remaining responsive to students' lived experiences.

INQUIRY FOCUS #1: REFLECTING ON IDENTITIES

What is gained when educators reflect on their self-described and ascribed identities?

We started our initial sessions with participants in the CRE-PD with an inquiry activity that provided educators several choices in deciding which of their identities they wanted to discuss. In so doing, we sought to address the anxiety in the room that emanated from asking educators to talk about themselves in ways that some had never been asked to do in a school environment. We invited educators to each make a web of circles and write their name in the center circle (see Figure 2.1). Educators were next prompted to think about words/phrases that described their identities. Specifically, we asked them to share "terms or descriptors that have been most helpful in shaping who you are and how you interact in the world." Finally, educators were asked to write words or phrases that others used to identify or ascribed to them.

While Latifah and Carmen shared their race/ethnicity as Black and Puerto Rican/Black, respectively, Rebekah did not share her racial/ethnic identity as White until she began to share her web in the activity about stereotypes (see Inquiry Focus #2). Many teachers of Color readily acknowledge

Figure 2.1. Teachers' Web of Identities

their racial/ethnic identity, whereas many White teachers do not feel that Whites have an ethnic culture until they find themselves in predominantly Black or culturally diverse communities. For instance, in Valli's (1995) study of three White preservice teachers, she argued that while the teachers tried to take a color-blind approach, they were forced to address issues of race as students of Color focused on their White skin, privilege, and perceived discriminatory pedagogical practices and lack of meaningful and productive teacher–student relationships.

In exploring the key features of culturally responsive teaching, Kozleski (2010) argues that teachers "need to explore their early experiences and family events that have contributed to their understanding of themselves as racial and nonracial beings. When teachers are able to come to terms with the historical shaping of their own identities and values, they can better relate to their colleagues and students who bring different histories" (p. 5). Moreover, their roles as educators/teachers, women/females, and daughters/mothers reveal how gender played a significant role in their lives. Similar to the experience Joanne described above, these inquiries into their web of identities opened up possibilities for educators to become critically aware of their own cultural identities. The exercise also created space for educators to consider detrimental stereotypes about their identities and to think critically about how others, including their students, might see them. Such critical reflection becomes extremely important as students, including Arnold and Hector in the class Joanne taught, seek ways to connect to their teachers by understanding educators' cultural histories as well (Achinstein & Aguirre, 2008).

Autobiographical Reflection—Michelle

At different professional development sessions, Michelle shared various aspects of her identities (see Figure 2.2). For example, in schools and educational experiences where there was a large student population of immigrants, she tended to foreground aspects of her racial and cultural identities that others might want to discuss with her. She is often asked, "Where are you from? No, really, where are you from?" Michelle grew up in a small town in Pennsylvania. Her father is Black and her ancestors on his side come from Nigeria. Her mother is White and her ancestors on her mother's side come from Italy. At any given moment, Michelle also is asked if she is Guatemalan in Oakland, California, or Dominican in New York City, and Indian in both geographical contexts given her phenotypic features. Having to continually negotiate people's varied constructions of her identities and cross-cultural educational experiences influences her understandings of how some immigrant students experience marginalization and injustices in their schooling and life experiences. Moreover, Michelle's initial interest in immigrant issues, especially students' constructions of their linguistic identities, stemmed from her prior experiences teaching English language learners from Ethiopia, Guatemala, and Vietnam in public middle and high schools in Oakland, California. Her current work with high school youth and graduate students across the educational life span who have emigrated from such countries as Nigeria, Ghana, and Cameroon continues to foreground students' negotiations of their multiple, intersecting identities of race, gender, class, skin color, immigrant status, and/or language status. For example, a high school student, Ibrahim, who recently emigrated from Nigeria, grew up speaking English with his family, community, and peers. English is the official language of Nigeria. In the after-school club where Michelle interacts with him, Ibrahim spoke English with the larger group and his African peers. However, we soon learned that he was put into an ESL class and we wondered how this was possible. We have to question whether perceptions of Ibrahim's cognitive ability are based on culturally based differences of his English pronunciation. Culturally relevant and sustaining educators who are aware of and value multiple accents of English, and the language differences among immigrant youth, can assist students in negotiating their complex linguistic identities and inappropriate placements in schools.

Many teachers described powerful "aha" moments from the ensuing conversations about their web of identities and the opportunities to "share our personal backgrounds and identities" (Barbara, White teacher, High School for Investigation and Inquiry, 3/31/2014). Tanya, a Black teacher, noted that "what was great to see was that even though [we were of] diverse cultures, we could share openly, we could empathize with one another with whatever came up in the conversations. So you got to know [your] colleagues on a nicer note as well" (Metropolitan High School, 4/9/2014). Yet, for others, tensions arose when teachers felt that conversations about race required too much work and would not change the fact that their experiences were different from those of their students. In particular, during a focus group

Figure 2.2. Michelle's Web of Identities: Self-identified/Ascribed

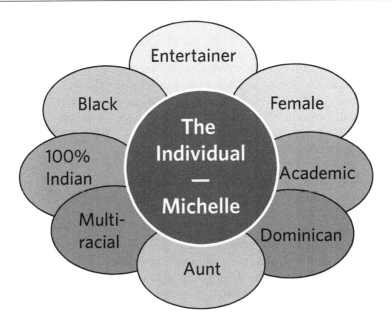

interview with five staff members, including three teachers, one guidance counselor, and an administrator, one educator remarked, "Some teachers don't want to put in the work because they think they are never going to relate to these kids" (Thorndike High School, Spring 2015). Perhaps these tensions emerged because all of the faculty within the school were required to participate in the CRE-PD, whether they sought to improve educational opportunity for students or not. For example, another staff member in the school remarked some participating educators did not seem to see "the value of making their curriculum and pedagogy more culturally relevant."

While conversations on race, equity, and pedagogy were difficult at times, the big "aha" moments came from allowing educators to push beyond emotional barriers of anxiety and fear to speak about race and other aspects of their identities. They began to understand themselves and their colleagues in a different way that allowed for the development of empathy regarding their colleagues and, in turn, their students. Equally important was building awareness that not all members of any particular group necessarily have the same experiences. So, while having a shared experience as a Latino male, for example, can provide access for connecting to students with the same background, adults need to also be aware of ways in which students' experiences are mediated by a variety of factors, such as race, gender, age, religion, and class (Jackson & Knight-Manuel, 2018; Wiedeman, 2002). Moreover, Gay (2010) advocated thinking of culture as an important facet of an individual's identity, not as a rigid determiner of how students will act and think. For example, several participants in the CRE-PD seemed surprised that the Black male student in a video we shared with them, *Tapping for Tuition* (Harris, 2012), enjoyed tap dancing so much; they expected Black teenage boys from Harlem to like hip-hop and assumed that most of their students would be engaged by hip-hop. We therefore attempted to utilize different videos of Black and Latinx youth throughout the CRE-PD to illuminate the heterogeneity of experiences within the same cultural group and to question what it means to be a teenager of Color. Yet for other teachers, the same video "struck a lot of emotions" (CRE interview, Gayle, Black, Metropolitan High School, 3/31/2014).

> There was one [video] in particular about a young man, an African young man, who was actually homeless here in New York. His family was in a shelter, but he went to college in Philly, but every weekend he would come back and he would dance on the train. And it was showing some of these kids . . . when you see them dancing and doing all these hat tricks and stuff. You know people will look at them like, "Oh, they're just panhandling and beggin' and so forth," but he was actually trying to work for that money . . . he saw the importance of school.

Gayle further noted that the video generated a lot of conversation among CRE-PD participants as they discussed how the experiences of the young man featured in the video were similar to the experiences of their own students. Culturally relevant teachers need opportunities to see and understand the varied lives youth live and how their lives are impacted by poverty and homelessness. These understandings allowed Gayle to be more empathetic about why a "child is coming to school late or what may be going on at home" that may affect the student's engagement in school.

INQUIRY FOCUS #2: EXAMINING EXPERIENCES

Write and share out about a stereotype that others have about you and how you negotiate living with this stereotype.

I guess it really was the subcultures. Being aware of that. It was really positive to think about stereotypes and how they really aren't true. We listed the positives that I think get lost. (Focus group interview, 4/2014)

We are some [of the] people who are the proponents of these very stereotypes. We must examine ourselves first as both Black and White. The reality is we come from homes in which many of the stereotypes are coming from; the Department of Education is scared of certain topics. It is a careful conversation because the students are not receiving these stereotypes from outside, they are receiving them when they come in the classroom (Bernard, Black teacher, Borough Academy, Observation, 11/5/2013)

Across the CRE-PD, we asked educators to work independently writing down responses to the following questions: Choose a time you encountered a stereotype about yourself that made you uncomfortable. What happened? How did you negotiate the stereotype? How, if at all, did the stereotype influence your ideas about yourself? What, if anything, did you do or think differently after this encounter? It quickly became apparent that many of the participants were able to relate and respond. However, there were educators who still felt that there were not differences between and among individuals and therefore found this to be a difficult conversation to engage in with their colleagues.

After reflecting, many educators shared their responses with the rest of the group, highlighting stereotypes they encountered that emerged across socioeconomic status, language, educational attainment, and family/community engagement. We were particularly hopeful that understanding their own responses would support their understandings of how they thought about their students.

Racial/Ethnic Identity and Socioeconomic Status

Some educators, particularly those who had experienced the negative effects of deficit-oriented stereotypes ascribed to them due to their cultural and/or linguistic identities, were eager to talk about how their race and/or ethnicity influenced their everyday lived experiences, especially since they worked in the contexts of school communities in New York City. Yet for other participants, particularly those from White, middle-class backgrounds who previously had not considered the role racial and/or ethnic stereotypes played in their lived experiences and interactions with culturally and linguistically diverse youth, this work was new. For Melissa, a teacher at Washington High School, stereotypes she encountered related to socioeconomic status were connected to her identity as a Black woman. She stated, for example, that she found it challenging to negotiate stereotypes about employment opportunities and job earnings. She shared:

One stereotype that bothers me is that people of Color, the best possible job they can reach is jobs in the public sector, because of the benefits. I have a big family. We have all sorts of different jobs. But the idea that that's all we can do. (Observation notes, 8/5/2013)

These understandings create an opportunity for Melissa to challenge deficit-oriented assumptions, informed by stereotypes about her race/ethnicity, about what she is capable of. In addition, implicit in Melissa's comments is an underlying frustration about what it feels like to encounter stereotypes that do not accurately reflect their lived experiences. These discussions provide opportunities for educators not only to voice their own frustrations with stereotypes they encounter, but also to consider how their students might feel frustrated when they encounter similar stereotypes.

Rebekah, a teacher at Metropolitan High School, was one of the few examples of a White teacher who could talk about her privilege in relation to the intersection of her identities as White, Jewish, and of a particular socioeconomic status. While many of the White educators who participated in the CRE-PD experienced challenges in naming negative stereotypes associated with their identities, Rebekah readily discussed how she often encountered stereotypes about money based on her Jewish identity. She shared: "People think because I'm Jewish I'm really cheap or rich." She went on to say that she did not perceive herself as wealthy, and wondered what led her students to assume that she was: "What makes you say that? Is it the color of my skin? The question of White privilege has to be addressed" (observation notes, 12/3/2013). Rebekah's naming of students' stereotypes related to her perceived socioeconomic status raised questions about White privilege among the educators present at the professional development session where the discussion took place. Laura asked what Rebekah meant when she used the phrase, "White privilege." Rebekah responded, defining White privilege as meaning that people may assume that because she is White, she has access and privilege that other White people have, even though she may not. Laura's question and Rebekah's response, positioning White privilege as advantages she may or may not have even though she is White, led us to understand that White educators with limited experience discussing issues of race, and the intersections of their multiple identities, power, and privilege, had differing, and sometimes limited, understandings of terms associated with those ideas.

For example, in another focus group interview, teachers remarked on how conversations about their identities allowed educators to share their diverse experiences and backgrounds in order to empathize with and connect to one another as well as their students. One teacher remarked:

> Just the privilege of being White. I grew up poor, my mom did not finish high school and my dad is from another country. But no matter how bad I had it, I always had the upper hand being White, being a female. I wanted to bridge that gap and I wanted to reach my students. (Mary, Focus group interview, 4/2014)

While Mary describes White privilege as benefiting her despite the socioeconomic challenges she encountered, as well as her mother's limited education and her father's immigrant status, her noting of "being a female" also is connected to notions of privilege. Both Mary and Rebekah illuminate the varied understandings of White privilege and the need for educators, particularly those who may be developing their understandings of their own identities, to discuss with colleagues what White privilege is. Talking about White privilege can be controversial. However, if not addressed, opportunities to create more-equitable schooling are lost. Kendall (2013) argues that "white privilege is an institutional (rather than personal) set of benefits granted to those of us, who by race, resemble the people who dominate the powerful positions in our institutions" (p. 1). Moreover, she contends that "all of us who are white, by race, have white privileges, although the extent to which we have them varies depending on our gender, sexual orientation, socioeconomic status, age, physical ability, size, and weight, and so on" (pp. 1–2). For example, she goes on to argue that when "looking at race and gender, we find that white men have greater access to power and resources than white women do" (p. 2). However, when we take into account how context and the intersection of identities matter, notions of privilege have to be re-examined. For example, research such as the Black Girls Matter Report (Crenshaw, Ocen, & Nanda, 2016) investigated the intersection of race and gender in K–12 schooling and highlighted how Black girls are disciplined, suspended, and expelled at a higher rate than White girls. Understanding notions of White privilege and the intersection of identities reveals the myriad ways in which gender and other social identity markers also mediate the experiences of both Black and White students and how they are treated in schools. Vaught and Castagno (2008) ask educators to consider how unpacking notions of White privilege must shift the focus to "the racial power inequities that structure institutions of schooling and the racial pattern of student school failure" (p. 99) and success. Educators who are aware of how their own multiple identities influence their lived experiences may better understand the importance of considering the role students' multiple, intersecting identities play in their access to learning opportunities, educational attainment, and the future job experiences they are afforded.

Educational Attainment and Race/Ethnic Identity

Across the CRE-PD, educators shared stereotypes others held of them related to expectations of their educational attainment and academic achievement based on their racial and ethnic identities. Two participants of Color, for example, talked about how their understandings of stereotypes others held of them changed over time. Kourtney and Talia described feeling as if they fit in with their White classmates growing up, and not feeling the pressure of negative stereotypes about their academic abilities until they enrolled in college. A teacher at Constitution High School, Kourtney shared in a whole-group discussion that she became aware of stereotypes about educational attainment after enrolling in college. She stated:

I'm Black and Latina, and a lot of times Black people are expected not to be as well educated. We're discussing our schooling and how we grew up. [I] went to a predominantly White school, [it was] all I knew, [I] never really felt that stereotype. In fact, I was a very great student. [It was] not until college when I learned about self-fulfilling prophecy and thought, I don't feel that way, but looking back on my experiences, as a child feeling like I had to fit into an environment that I wasn't really part of. I'm trying to dissect that. (Observation notes, 8/5/2013)

Kourtney's comments simultaneously made visible tensions in her negotiation of others' expectations for her academic achievement, even as she described not experiencing those tensions as a student in a predominantly White high school. Moreover, Kourtney's statement that she is "trying to dissect that" points to the continuous work involved in analyzing one's own experience with stereotypes (Ford & Dillard, 1996).

In addition to supporting educators' own recognition and negotiation of stereotypes others held of their educational attainment, the inquiry activity also created opportunities for developing the sociopolitical awareness of White educators who previously might not have understood how stereotypes influenced the experiences and perspectives of their colleagues of Color. Talia, also a teacher at Constitution High School, shared the following experience:

I was always mixed with White people and they never saw me as different, or I never saw myself as different. But this one experience, being Jamaican, we are expected to be this promiscuous group of people who like reggae. I had this one experience in college where I had to work with other people in a research center. [I] had a presentation coming up, [and a female professor] wrote me an email saying that she was looking forward to it and also that I should brush my hair. Like, really? I needed a reminder to brush my hair? . . . It's even sad to be reminded of that, the stereotype of Black hair and how we groom ourselves. I never went back. This great research opportunity and this whole application process. I probably missed out on a great opportunity. (Observation notes, 8/5/2013)

Talia's decision to not return to the research team provides insight into the negative impact stereotypes about race and ethnicity have in students' educational experiences. Again, educators' reflections on their experiences with stereotypes create entry points for considering how youth of Color may negotiate stereotypes across schooling contexts and educational opportunity.

Language

Educators also shared their experiences navigating stereotypes based on the languages they spoke or others' assumptions about their racial, ethnic, and linguistic identities. For example, Shuvanna, a teacher at Borough Academy, shared that her Arabic Muslim identity was not easily read by those who did not know her. She shared, "I don't look the part, but I am Arabic Muslim . . . I am Arabic, I speak Arabic" (observation notes, 11/5/2013). She shared that until people realized she spoke Arabic, they did not recognize "who their company was." Andrew, a Latino teacher at Transformation Academy, discussed navigating similar experiences. He shared, "The idea that all Hispanics are Mexican or Puerto Rican, and [people] don't know the difference. I'm mixed, but I'm not Mexican or Puerto Rican. The other thing, that I don't speak Spanish. Hispanics come to me and speak Spanish and I'm like, really? I was born here" (observation notes, 8/5/13). A third teacher, Emily, described having people not recognize her Dominican identity even though she was fluent in both Spanish and English. She described how her older sister almost was placed into special education classes inappropriately because she experienced academic challenges due to language differences she encountered after moving from the Dominican Republic to the United States and enrolling in school. A teacher at Amsterdam High School discussed how "her accent sounds as a Hispanic in the United States. Her sister was "not getting credit for the fact that she is educated" (5/29/2014).

These educators demonstrate how considerations of stereotypes related to racial, ethnic, and linguistic identities can easily hinder or facilitate students' access to educational opportunity. Culturally relevant and sustaining pedagogies call for educators to better understand how students come to school speaking multiple languages and are already engaging in varied forms of linguistic dexterity, and that there is a great need for such dexterity to be a part of the curriculum (Allen, Jackson, & Knight, 2012; Paris & Alim, 2017).

Family/Community Engagement

A fourth area of focus that emerged when educators discussed stereotypes they encountered was related to family and community involvement. These stereotypes were voiced primarily by educators of Color who shared that their lived experiences were not reflective of deficit-oriented stereotypes held of them, their family members, and those in their communities. Paula, for example, discussed deficit-oriented stereotypes of Black males and their families. She said:

> [That] stereotype of the Black male who doesn't know how many children he has, who doesn't support them financially, emotionally,

like a nonexistent sperm donor, an abuser, just a really nasty person. . . . Growing up, fathers were the ones who were mowing the lawns. I don't have people I know who are deadbeat dads. I would almost challenge people to name two deadbeat dads who are Black. It's like Maury, Jerry Springer, and Oprah got together to brainwash them all. I fight back with these mentoring programs to have amazing males come into our schools. [I] had a police sergeant, who happens to be my cousin, come in to talk to the kids. (Observation notes, 8/5/2013)

In addition to demonstrating that her lived experiences do not reflect deficit-oriented stereotypes of Black males as being absent financially and emotionally, Paula challenges these stereotypes by inviting "amazing males" to talk with her students as mentors. Similarly, Dominic discusses a misalignment between his experiences as Black father and stereotypes about Black males:

I live it. When I'm with my daughters, people either look at me and smile, like, that's what's up, or they look at you like, wow, that's what's up. I agree, debunking the whole thing that the person I am is hood, that when I'm dressed down I could potentially be a drug dealer who likes fast cars and fast women—not really. I got a laundry list of brothers who are just like me. I'm in a fraternity, I could circle up 80 guys who have the same morals and beliefs, hard workers, professionals, certified, degree, who can debunk that particular stereotype. . . . There is some truth to some of this stuff. The same dudes I see on Manning Street in the morning when I leave are the same dudes I see on Manning Street when I get back. (Observation notes, 8/5/2013)

Dominic's comments point to the tension he experiences in navigating negative stereotypes about his role as a father and about Black men in his community.

Educators' willingness to talk openly about stereotypes they encounter created a collaborative space within the professional development sessions that allowed participants not only to share their own experiences, but also to learn from the experiences shared by other educators present. Lisa, a White female teacher at Borough Academy, for example, shared that prior to participating in the CRE-PD she had not actively considered how her cultural identity influenced her work with Black and Latinx youth. Specifically, she noted that the opportunity to engage with educators from racial and ethnic backgrounds different from her own encouraged her to think differently about her work:

I think of myself [as]White only when I come here and I am a minority. Because I am in the minority. I have travelled to other countries where I am the minority and it is a totally different thing. (Observation notes, 11/5/2013)

The stereotypes educators discussed across contexts of socioeconomic status, language, educational attainment, and family/community engagement accomplished two main purposes. First, educators engaged in the important practice of self-reflection. Second, they were made aware of stereotypes their colleagues encountered and negotiated, which, in turn, created opportunities to consider experiences similar to and different from their own. The activity served as a rich starting point for shifting discussions about stereotypes that educators experienced in their own lives to those they may have held about students, their families, and their communities. Those stereotypes, and educators' shifting considerations of them, and the strengths of Black and Latino young men are discussed in the remainder of this chapter.

CONNECTION TO CLASSROOMS, SCHOOL CULTURE, AND COLLEGE ACCESS

Focus on Curriculum and Teaching

Research exploring the role of cultural and academic identities demonstrates the importance of teachers' rigorous content practices in all subject areas (Knight & Marciano, 2013; Mensah & Jackson, 2018; Milner, 2017) and of enacted positive beliefs about students' potential, especially in such areas as math (Ramirez & Celedon-Pattichis, 2012) and science (Moore, 2008). Questioning the underlying beliefs and assumptions surrounding "who can do math and science" is essential to understanding and supporting the development of dispositions toward and enactments of culturally relevant pedagogical practices. Donna, for example, shared that she was one of two students of Color in a college chemistry class of more than 250 students. Due to the limited number of Black women in STEM fields, Donna noted, "people find it strange [that I am] a Black, female, Haitian math teacher" (observation notes, 2013). Designing culturally relevant learning environments includes incorporating students' culture as an asset to their success. For example, in supporting students of Color in seeing themselves as mathematicians, one of the teachers in our study created a bulletin board highlighting famous Black and Latinx mathematicians. The teacher also assigned students to write about why it is important to study mathematicians of Color (see Figure 2.3).

Figure 2.3. Teacher's Bulletin Board, "Why Is It Important to Study Mathematicians of Color?"

As Milner (2017) notes, "The idea of seeing oneself in the curriculum and through instruction helps students understand the important ways in which their culture has contributed to various content areas and within society" (p. 11) and that they too can take up careers in these fields. For example, as the recent film *Hidden Figures* (Melfi, 2016) demonstrated, Black women such as Katherine Johnson and Mary Jackson worked at the National Aeronautics and Space Administration (NASA) during the space race, the Cold War rivalry between the United States and Soviet Union.

Focus on School Culture

How does the school community see the representation of students within the entire school culture? One way that teachers and administrators can focus on student learning is to examine whose student work is portrayed throughout the school. Annie from Exploratory High School explained that during an evening CRE-PD session when educators from multiple schools shared their action plans with one another, she decided to engage her colleagues in a walk inside the school as part of her action plan to begin enacting culturally relevant practices. She noted:

We did a gallery walk of the bulletin boards, assessing representations of Black and Latino males at our school and the mission statement. We asked, "How do we represent ourselves?" We counted student work and broke it down by gender. There were 160 pieces of student work. Thirty percent boys to 70% girls that were represented on these bulletin boards, so that's something interesting in terms of how you represent your students. (Observation, 2013)

What does this image convey about young men and their learning and achievement? Harper's (2015) work argues for ways that teachers, school leaders, and students can show, document, and explain the success of Black and Latino males through visual images throughout a school. Spencer, Noll, Stolzfus, and Harpalani (2001, as cited in Harper, 2015) "argue that students of color who are exposed to positive messages about themselves, their schools, and their communities often develop healthier identities and higher educational aspirations" (p. 163).

Focus on College and Career Readiness

In the pursuit of college and career readiness, culturally relevant and sustaining educators emphasize high expectations and affirmations of students' identities. At a time when college and career readiness continues to be positioned as one of the goals of secondary education, we recognize the importance of explicitly connecting what we learned from educators' participation in the CRE-PD to students' postsecondary opportunities. For example, fieldtrips to colleges facilitated culturally relevant and sustaining pedagogies by creating opportunities for students to build and strengthen their cultural competence and examine educational content. At the same time, college visits further supported youth's educational experiences by linking the co-curricular activities of college trips to larger sociopolitical realities experienced by youth of Color. Many of the teachers across the 28 high schools we collaborated with took students on fieldtrips to visit college campuses. Applying a culturally relevant approach to college visits supported youth and their teachers in visiting campuses attended by students of Color rather than only predominantly White institutions, creating opportunities for youth of Color to be viewed as college bound.

For example, Wesley, one teacher from Golden Ridge Community High School, took students on a 5-night college tour in the southern United States. Wesley and his students visited several historically Black colleges and universities (HBCUs), including Morehouse College, Clark Atlanta University, Virginia State University, and Howard University. The group also visited the National Great Blacks in Wax Museum in Baltimore and the Natural Museum of African American History and Culture. Wesley spoke passionately about students seeing themselves in the college students on campus.

In a CRE-PD session, Wesley said he planned the trip because he wanted to highlight cultural aspects of Black history and how those aspects related to students' lives. In providing opportunities for students to see contributions Black people made to society, in addition to participating in college tours, Wesley noted his desires for students to ask, "If I were to apply to college now would I be prepared for this?" Moreover, Wesley asked students to complete a survey before they left for the 5-day trip, requiring them to research the demographics, tuition, and sports teams available at each college. A scavenger hunt activity further called for students to generate thought-provoking questions they could ask while participating in the trip (Observation, 2/28/2013).

Kacy and Rosemary, two educators from one of the technical schools, similarly sought to take their students on a college tour that built upon students' cultural experiences and racial identities as strengths. They organized a trip for students to travel from New York City to Maryland to visit the campus of Morgan State University. The educators shared that they chose to visit Morgan State because it appealed to students who wanted to travel out of state for college, but not travel too far away from home. In addition, Kacy and Rosemary shared that the university's tuition was "reasonable," and degrees offered included bachelors, masters, and doctorate. Morgan State also provided support services to low-income, first-generation students as well as students who were English language learners (observation notes, 2/28/2013).

Even as educators across the CRE-PD sought to expose students to HBCUs, we found that teachers often were less aware of colleges identified as Hispanic-serving institutions, such as City College of New York, Bronx Community College, Lehman College, and Queens College (www. hacu.net/assnfe/CompanyDirectory.asp?). These institutions participate in a federal program that assists colleges or universities that enroll a majority of first-generation, low-income Hispanic students. These are colleges that educators should consider visiting with youth, particularly Latinx students.

CONCLUSION

Before educators are able to fully engage in an examination of how stereotypes and deficit thinking about Black and Latino young men influence their work with youth, they must negotiate understandings of their own racial and ethnic identities (Marx, 2008; Pollock, Deckman, Mira, & Shalaby, 2010). For example, Ford and Dillard (1996) argue:

> We must engage in reflective activities as teachers in order to understand the present versions of ourselves and our actions, as shaped by our past experiences, and to ultimately guide our aspirations for the future. In other words, we must bring

to conscious examination our historical selves, which will allow us to deconstruct our present self in order to gain knowledge of self as subject. (p. 237)

As teachers and school leaders took up opportunities to engage in critical self-reflection about their racial/ethnic identities and cultural backgrounds, they were able to see some of the similarities and differences among themselves. They were able to see the ways in which their experiences and those of their colleagues have been shaped historically, politically, and culturally. Moreover, more-caring and empathetic understandings of the stereotypes that they each encountered enabled them to get to know one another in more humanizing ways. Chapter 3 will discuss providing opportunities for further critical reflection on how teachers' identities and cultural backgrounds impact their pedagogical practices with students from diverse backgrounds.

QUESTIONS AND ACTIONS FOR INDIVIDUALS AND SMALL GROUPS WITHIN SCHOOL COMMUNITIES

1. Create a web of identities. What does this reveal about you? What do you think it reveals about how your colleagues see you? What do you think it reveals about how your students see you?
2. Make a list of stereotypes people hold about your race/ethnicity. Reflect on how you became aware of those stereotypes. For example, encounters in the media, with others, including students, parents, etc. How have you responded to those stereotypes? Which aspects of your identities are more likely to be stereotyped in negative ways? In positive ways? Which stereotypes are you in conversation with others about? Why or why not?
3. What kinds of support would you need to engage members of your school community in discussions of race? Does your district provide any professional development or resources around culturally relevant and sustaining practices and racial identity work? How could you present the idea of piloting a small professional learning community on culturally relevant and sustaining practices to your principal or district leaders?

CHAPTER 3

Challenging Stereotypes, Supporting Students' Strengths

Inquiry Focus: How can educators working with youth of Color become aware of and challenge deficit-oriented stereotypes of their students?

Opportunity: Educators can engage in uncovering and challenging stereotypes while building on their students' strengths.

I think the boys don't really have like a, I don't want to say a role model . . . but they don't have a whole lot of examples that they can point to. When they think of a successful Black or Latino male, they think Jay Z or LeBron James. That's the culture that they have. And it's nothing against the boys, it's just what they see out there and they don't see anything else. Now we have Barack Obama, that's an easy one to point to . . . but there isn't much else. (Jennifer, White female educator)

Youth of Color continue to confront deficit-oriented stereotypes about who they are and what they can achieve. Negative portrayals of Black and Latino young men, for example, permeate local and national news media, and popular culture representations of urban communities, even as the Black Lives Matter movement calls attention to injustices encountered by people of Color. At the same time, national political rhetoric has negatively positioned Black, Latinx, and immigrant communities, particularly those situated in urban centers, as places plagued by crime where innocent people are in danger even as they walk down the street (Corasaniti, 2016). These stereotypes, and others like them, may negatively influence educators' perceptions of the diverse students, families, and communities with whom they work. As a result, we examine how educators working with youth of Color may become aware of and challenge deficit-oriented stereotypes of their students and build on their strengths in culturally relevant ways that support student learning and achievement.

To support us in our inquiry, we highlight the perspectives of educators as they identified and negotiated their understandings of the lived experiences of youth of Color, specifically the Black and Latino male students, with whom they work. We make visible the tensions educators encountered in identifying and describing assumptions about their students, examine how those assumptions are grounded in deficit-oriented stereotypes prevalent in U.S. society, and consider opportunities for shifting to asset-based considerations of Black and Latino young men across educational contexts.

It has been well documented that educators' perceptions, attitudes, and dispositions toward their students can facilitate or hinder students' learning, achievement, and access to higher education (Allen, 2015; Douglas, Lewis, Douglas, Scott, & Garrison-Wade, 2008; Milner, 2016; Rogers & Way, 2016). For example, in the quotation that opens this chapter, Jennifer says that her Black and Latino male students do not have exposure to role models beyond musicians, athletes, or former President Obama. Jennifer's perspective fails to acknowledge the existence of Black and Latino men connected to students' lived experiences who serve as role models for them, such as family members, educators, clergy, and community members (Knight, Norton, Bentley, & Dixon, 2004). Rather than connect these role models to the educational experiences of youth, Jennifer's perspective leads to missed opportunities for creating more culturally relevant learning environments for students.

In this chapter, we enact an inquiry approach to name and understand the stereotypes, challenges, and strength-based assets, in research and those that educators were aware of—and may themselves hold—of culturally and linguistically diverse youth. We draw connections between these expectations of youth and teachers' enactment of instructional practices, institutional policies, and informal learning contexts that lead to facilitating and/or hindering equitable educational opportunities, including college readiness and access, for youth of Color, specifically Black and Latino young men.

EVERYDAY PRACTICES IN CONTEXT

Even as today's teachers encounter messages in the mainstream media and popular culture about the importance of valuing Black lives and taking action to support social justice, students in classrooms across the United States continue to experience education as disconnected from, if not detrimental to, their identities as youth of Color. Moreover, teachers who seek to educate students in an equitable manner may not be aware of how they could modify their existing practices to better support their students (Knight-Manuel et al., 2016).

In our work with educators over the years, we have encountered multiple instances when teachers who "mean well" contribute to educational inequities through their interactions with students of Color, their families, and their communities. Take, for example, Ms. Vasquez, a Latina teacher who is well-regarded in her school community and considers herself an advocate for her students who challenges them to meet high expectations for academic achievement. One afternoon, Ms. Vasquez refused to allow three Black 10th-graders, Dwight, James, and Kevin, to enter the classroom and take a test being given to their classmates because they did not arrive on time (Watson, 2016). Ms. Vasquez explained in a written behavior log that since the young men chose to continue playing basketball in the school gym for several minutes after their lunch period ended, they should be held accountable for consequently arriving late to class by being denied the opportunity to take the test. Ms. Vasquez also noted that the students would not be provided with another opportunity to take the test and would each receive a grade of zero, to hold them accountable for their actions.

While Ms. Vasquez may have believed that Dwight, James, and Kevin were more likely to arrive in class on time in the future as a result of missing the test, her actions concern us. First, tests typically are used as assessments to provide teachers insight into students' understandings of the concepts being studied so that future instruction can be modified to support student learning. Since Dwight, James, and Kevin did not take the test, Ms. Vasquez was not able to use the test results to differentiate her instruction for them in the same way that she would have for the rest of the students in the class. The young men's punishment resulted in inequitable access to the educational opportunities afforded their classmates, not to mention a low class grade that did not reflect their understanding of class content.

Second, we wonder about the role race and gender played in Ms. Vasquez's refusal to allow Dwight, James, and Kevin to enter the class and take the test. Young Black men continue to be disproportionately disciplined in school contexts (Losen, Hodson, Keith, Morrison, & Belway, 2015). Moreover, young Black men who play basketball often encounter stereotypes that position them as valuing athletics over academics (Benson, 2000). Had the three late students been Asian, Latina, Native American, or White young women who lost track of time while reading in the school library, we wonder whether Ms. Vasquez would have similarly denied them entry to the classroom and the opportunity to take the test.

Further, Ms. Vasquez's actions raise questions for us about how Dwight, James, and Kevin are perceived by students and adults within the larger school community. To their peers seated inside the classroom taking the test, Dwight, James, and Kevin could be seen as disengaged. For the adults who saw the three young men walking around the school building instead of seated in class, negative perceptions of them as off-task or not valuing their education could be reinforced. Finally, the young men may be less likely to attend Ms. Vasquez's class in the future if they believe they are unwelcome there, or that Ms. Vasquez does not think they are worthy of her efforts to teach them.

We do not share our concerns about the interaction between Ms. Vasquez and Dwight, James, and Kevin in an attempt to characterize Ms. Vasquez as an uncaring or ineffective teacher, or the young men as stellar students. We know that a brief anecdote cannot capture the nuances of relationships between students and their teachers, or the context of their work together. However, we are interested in considering whether and how Ms. Vasquez might have held the students accountable for their actions in a more culturally relevant way that would not have interrupted their access to educational opportunity. Further, our own work with teachers and students in multiple contexts spanning several decades supports our understanding that Ms. Vasquez is not alone in thinking she is supporting her students by holding what she may consider to be high expectations for their timely arrival in class when, actually, she is contributing to their inequitable access to educational opportunity. We are left with the following question: How might teachers be supported in questioning simplistic and singular notions about youth of Color, challenging stereotypes, and building upon the assets youth bring with them into their schooling experiences?

INQUIRY FOCUS #1: CHALLENGING SINGULAR NOTIONS ABOUT CULTURALLY DIVERSE YOUTH

How can educators challenge simplistic, singular notions about culturally and linguistically diverse youth?

We found that an effective approach for engaging educators in critical reflection about their assumptions about students involved asking educators to identify, describe, and, as we will discuss in the next section of this chapter, challenge dominant stereotypes about people of Color prevalent in our society. Identifying and publicly naming negative stereotypes may be difficult for educators, particularly those who are not used to talking about issues of race and identity, and do not want to offend their colleagues by repeating negative stereotypes. To facilitate discussion, we shared our own stories of times when we made assumptions based on deficit-oriented stereotypes. In the process, we made ourselves vulnerable to critique just as we invited educators to do the same as they reflected on their own perspectives and what informs those perspectives (see Michelle's Autobiographical Reflection in this chapter).

We also guided educators through a shared viewing and discussion of Chimamanda Adichie's video *The Danger of a Single Story* (2009). In the video, Adichie, who is Nigerian, discussed how people in Europe and the United States view and promote certain images of Africa and Africans. For example, she shared: "I, too, would think that Africa was a place of beautiful landscapes, beautiful animals, and incomprehensible people, fighting sense-less wars, dying of poverty and AIDS, unable to speak for themselves and waiting to be saved by a kind, White foreigner." She further discussed her own internalization about Africans who were poor, like Fide, a boy who worked in her family's home and lived in a nearby village with his own family. Adichie had a single story about Africans living in poverty and was therefore surprised, after interacting with Fide's family one day, to realize that they could make baskets that were beautiful and of great value. Adichie emphasized how if we are taught one thing about a people for long enough, we begin to believe it. She also drew attention to her travels in Mexico and how she had become complicit in buying into the single story of the U.S. perspective of the abject Mexican immigrant.

After watching the video, educators responded to Adichie's perspective, considering whether and how they might make similar assumptions and judgments about students of Color and their families, particularly in in-stances when educators might not interact with members of cultural, lin-guistic, and socioeconomic groups that differ from their own. Michelle also shared her own struggle to navigate the tension she encountered after her brother told her years ago that he was gay and she was forced to recognize and confront her own negative assumptions.

Autobiographical Reflection—Michelle

After viewing the Adichie video, I reinforced how all of us are complicit in our thoughts and actions toward various cultural groups. I shared with teachers how I unknowingly had picked up negative messages about gay people while growing up in a conventional Christian home in a small town in Pennsylvania. When I first went to California in the early 1980s, my brother shared that he would tell me something after I had been in California for a year. Perhaps he thought that living in California would prepare me for his news. However, when my younger brother eventually told me he was gay, I cried on his shoulder and told him that he could never marry or have children. How wrong was I? Interestingly enough, many states have since passed the Marriage Equality Act and over the years my brother has married and had two children.

While several educators remarked on how important it was to tell such stories of my family members, rarely did any of the educators in schools discuss the intersection of race, gender, and sexual orientation of Black and Latinx LGBTQ youth. At City Leadership Academy, the stereotype that "girls who play sports are gay" was mentioned and not challenged. Moreover, Laura, an educator at Metropolitan High School, noted a couple of different times that in the case of Latinos, "no one wants talk about the homosexual boys." They remain invisible. Only one of the schools that we visited had curriculum and extracurricular activities to support LGBTQ youth. The lack of attention to the intersection of Black and Latino young men's identities gives rise to missed opportunities to recognize, embrace, and affirm the complexity of their identities, build on their assets, and support their educational experiences in schools (Pennell, 2016).

During one discussion, after watching the Adichie video and listening as Michelle shared her reflection on the assumptions she made after her brother told her he was gay, a group of four White teachers at Buena Vista High School reflected on their preference for being gently led to consider how they might interpret and/or send negative messages about the cultural groups their students belong to; this method helped alleviate their anxiety about being considered racist for talking explicitly about their assumptions. Moreover, Jamie, a White female principal at Occupational Prep Academy, shared her discomfort with realizing that, just as Adichie pitied Fide and his family for living in an African village even as they created priceless baskets, she felt she might be "pitying" students of Color living in low-income neighborhoods, and not providing instruction at levels that challenged them. This process of critical reflection allowed teachers and administrators to realize that everyone has learned stereotypes, directly or indirectly, from a variety of sources, such as popular media and their own familial experiences.

Yet even as we asked educators to name prevalent stereotypes that fore-ground deficit-oriented notions about youth of Color, their families, and their communities, our intent is not for teachers to conclude that these beliefs are acceptable. Rather, similar to Gonzalez and Ayala-Alcantar (2008), we advocate working toward creating a space for teachers to discuss negative beliefs and stereotypes regarding Latinx youth. We support teachers in the process of challenging these deficit-oriented beliefs by acknowledging first that these beliefs about students of Color exist, and then that by naming these beliefs, educators can better understand how they may be hindering students' learning and achievement.

INQUIRY FOCUS #2: CHALLENGING STEREOTYPES TO UNDERSTAND ASSETS

How can educators challenge stereotypes and understand youth's assets?

Our work with teachers also has led us to understand the importance of providing time for small-group discussion as a way to support educators in transitioning from talking about broader societal stereotypes to considering actual assumptions they hold about students of Color, their families, and their communities—and how those assumptions may translate into classroom practices that are not culturally relevant. Small groups allow for interactive participation among teachers, who may be more likely to share their personal experiences than in a larger group. We asked educators to form groups of four or five and to list on chart paper what they saw as societal perceptions of Black and Latino males.

Educators told us they found it difficult at first to name these stereotypes, because they worried their colleagues might think that the stereotypes were personally held beliefs. However, after talking collectively about widely held societal beliefs, educators worked together to name stereotypes their students of Color encountered on a daily basis, generating a variety of responses (see Figure 3.1 for examples from nine small groups across multiple school communities). The lists generated across the nine small groups focused on negative stereotypes, as educators drew upon what they saw in popular media images, including news broadcasts, television programs, movies, and music. Perhaps due to a discomfort in moving from naming stereotypes verbally to putting them to paper, some groups' written lists did not capture the nuances of their small-group conversations. Even so, words such as *aggressive*, *criminals*, *lazy*, *homophobic*, *not intelligent*, *scary*, *low expectations*, and *thug* were among those written by educators. The Metropolitan High School served a high immigrant population, and when stereotypes in regard to Black immigrants arose, the notion emerged that African immigrants had a thick accent in contrast to Caribbean immigrants. Rosa and Flores (2017) contend that often how one's accent is received is situated in raciolinguistic views that conflate race and linguistic deficiency, and, in turn, do not sustain students' language assets.

Figure 3.1. Stereotypes of Black and Latino Young Men Identified in Small Groups Across Multiple School Communities

Aggressive	Homophobic	Scary
Criminals	Narrow aspirations (sports, rapping)	Aggressive
Moochers		Thug
Player	Criminals	
Chauvinist	Lazy	
	Not intelligent	
Lack diversity (socioeconomic, cultural, aspirational)	Gangsta	Not family men
Poverty	Low expectations	"Fatherless" upbringing
	Tough guys	

Unfortunately, the educators' responses did not surprise us. Many of the stereotypes listed reflect those found in popular culture, and analyzed in educational research literature. They are consistent with notions of academic disengagement—lazy, low expectations, anti-intellectual, and having narrow aspirations—often associated with stereotypes of Black and Latino young men. Some stereotypes, such as aggressive, scary, criminal, and thug, highlighted a fear of Black and Latino young men (Cammarota, 2004; James, 2012; Lopez, 2012); others blamed students' families for their lack of educational motivation and goals (Carey, 2016; Gonzales, 2012).

It was far more difficult for educators to identify and describe assets typically associated with Black and Latino young men prevalent in U.S. society. We called these assets "(in)visible strengths" to reflect their frequent absence in popular culture and challenged teachers to work in their small groups to make visible as many of the strengths they see in their own students as they could. This proved to be easier for educators from some school communities than for others, who shared that they were not used to thinking about young Black and Latino men in this way.

We continued to encourage educators in their small groups to think through their daily interactions with young men of Color in their school communities and to reflect on qualities of Black and Latino young men that they rarely see in the media. After a while, lists were generated that included the following items: resilient, protective, curious, and motivated (see Figure 3.2). While we agree with educators that those characteristics often are perceived as strengths that may not always be visible, some of the items listed have deficit-oriented stereotypes embedded within them. For example, one group described Black and Latino young men as able to "successfully function within different cultures at home and in school." The statement provided an entry point for us to ask educators what it looks like to "successfully" navigate these different cultures, and to consider how and why those differences exist in the first place. Another group responded that Black and Latino young men are "aware of society's prejudices and biases," drawing positive attention to the young men's sociopolitical consciousness. These responses provide a valuable opportunity for shifting the conversation from considerations of damaging stereotypes that exist in society, toward discussions of how these stereotypes influence our own work with youth of Color in our classrooms and school communities.

In analyzing teachers' conceptions of the Black and Latino young men they teach, more-nuanced and contradictory notions came forth. In many instances, educators' conceptions reflected the three tenets of culturally relevant pedagogy outlined by Ladson-Billings (2011). For example, educators noted the first tenet, related to student learning and achievement, in describing strengths such as "focused on academic abilities," "emotional intelligence," "high achieving," "motivated/ambitious," "intelligent" and "curious." The second tenet, highlighting critical competence and/or the

Figure 3.2. (In)Visible Strengths of Black and Latino Young Men Identified in Small Groups Across Multiple School Communities

Resilient Sensitivity Motivated/ambitious Respect for elders Protective	Sensitive, thoughtful, kind Critical about their own culture Respectful Curious Intelligent Adaptability (navigating identities, relationships)	Aware of society's prejudices and biases
Ability to impose their culture on a majority Successfully function within different cultures at home and in school	Masking weaknesses and vulnerabilities Resilience/loyalty	Tough exterior as coping mechanism Survival instincts
Often, their responsibilities at home illustrate their devotion to family.	High achieving Sensitivity Curiosity	Stability Loyalty/trust

cultural and linguistic dexterity of Black and Latino young men, was revealed by educators who recognized how youth were able to navigate school and home cultures, successfully function within different cultures at home and in school, and navigate multiple identities. The third tenet focuses on the critical awareness or sociopolitical consciousness of students. The teachers noted how their Black and Latino male students were aware of society's prejudice and biases and were critical about their own culture.

Notions of the importance of family, loyalty/trust, respect for elders, and devotion to family were recognized as being rooted in cultural values, providing strengths-based observations of Black and Latino young men in contrast to deficit-oriented notions depicting them as lazy and disrespectful. One educator noted "the young men's ability to impose their culture on the majority" (e.g., music), which reflects the love–hate relationship that many educators have with Black and Latinx youth and hip-hop culture, for instance (Ladson-Billings, 2011). Many teachers also noted the resilience of many Black and Latino young men and how they mask their weaknesses and vulnerabilities as a mechanism for survival. On the subject of the resilience of African American families, as suggested by McCubbin and colleagues (as cited in Ungar, 2005), "daily functioning amidst negative realities requires a high level of motivation, commitment, tenacity and creativity" (p. xxvi). This understanding of resiliency contradicts the view of Black and Latino young men as unmotivated, especially in school. Thoughtful and kind are descriptions that we rarely see mentioned about Black and Latino young men.

The inquiry-oriented activities described above create opportunities for teachers to share their perceptions and understandings of Black and Latino young men. Critically reflecting upon stereotypes and invisible strengths of youth allows teachers to personalize their views from their own interactions with youth in their schools. Seeing their views of Black and Latino young men in their own interactions and practices challenges negative stereotypes and deficit thinking about students. Specifically, educators reveal a more complex understanding of their identities, academic promise, and social potential. Asset-oriented pedagogical practices can be implemented in your context as you think about the deficit-oriented stereotypes held about your varied school populations, such as African English language learners, Latina girls in science, or Black young men in special education.

INQUIRY FOCUS #3: CREATING MORE-EQUITABLE EDUCATIONAL PRACTICES

How can educators create schoolwide structures that support more-equitable educational practices for students of Color?

In considering how educators may move toward imagining and implementing more-equitable educational practices for the Black and Latino young men with whom they work that build on students' invisible strengths, we return to Jennifer's statement at the beginning of this chapter. In noting that her students do not have Black and Latino male role models besides Jay-Z, LeBron James, and former President Obama, Jennifer creates an opportunity for considering how educators' assumptions may begin to be challenged. For example, Jennifer's assumption that the Black and Latino young men enrolled in her school "don't have a whole lot of examples [of role models] that they can point to" foregrounded stereotypes of celebrities as the only role models relevant to the young men's experiences and futures. Moreover, in saying ". . . they don't see anything else," Jennifer assumed that the youth were not aware of or familiar with Black and Latino men in their families, schools, and communities who could be considered role models. She continued her comment, saying:

> For Summer Bridge we brought in this random lawyer and he is so inspiring. And I think those kids will remember that, that speech he gave, for a while. I don't know if that's the answer . . . but um,

somehow giving them some other examples. 'Cause they have the right idea . . . I want to become successful . . . I want to make it out of the streets . . . I want to be someone . . . but that's who they're looking at.

In considering the Black lawyer who visited with students as "random" rather than connected to students' lived experiences, Jennifer further demonstrated the tension she experienced in envisioning successful Black males as being connected to the students she works with. Additionally, in imagining students as thinking, "I want to make it out of the streets," Jennifer used language often complicit in popular media stereotypes of Black and Latinx youth as needing to leave their communities to experience "success." Moreover, Jennifer's statement that students "have the right idea" in saying, "I want to be someone," assumed that the identities youth currently are embodying do not make them "someone." Such a focus on future-oriented identities fails to acknowledge and value characteristics youth currently possess and bring with them into the classroom every day.

We encourage educators to talk directly with youth about their experiences and perspectives, in order to better understand youth's nuanced and distinct identities, influences, and aspirations. For example, talking with young men about the people in their lives whom they consider role models creates opportunities for youth to challenge Jennifer's stereotypes that the only males who inspire them are famous musicians, athletes, or politicians that they do not actually have physical access to. One way we encouraged educators to identify existing role models in the lives of their students was to think back to their own experiences growing up and name a person who inspired excellence within them. They wrote of parents, teachers, and extended family members, realizing that their own students may have similar role models.

CONNECTING TO CLASSROOMS, SCHOOL CULTURE, AND COLLEGE ACCESS

In the sections that follow, we highlight three strategies educators enacted to create more-equitable educational practices that drew on the invisible strengths of students across contexts of curriculum and instruction, school culture, and college readiness and access. Each strategy provided a practical way for educators to build on the tenets of culturally relevant pedagogy— student learning and achievement, cultural competence, and sociopolitical consciousness—in ways that challenged deficit-oriented stereotypes about and built on the strengths of youth.

Focus on Curriculum and Teaching

In seeking to build on students' experiences while connecting to curriculum and instruction, several educators mentioned that they took materials from the CRE-PD back to their classes, while others modified their lesson and unit plans by building on lessons learned throughout the professional development series. For example, Mr. Parsons, a teacher at the High School for Reform and Innovation, built on the invisible strengths of his students when he created opportunities for them to connect a literary analysis lesson with their engagement with poetry outside of the classroom. Mr. Parsons modified a lesson he taught in previous years to intentionally include poems written by or focused on people of Color, and invited students to bring in poems they were interested in analyzing. As a result, students read poems written by Langston Hughes, Juan Felipe Herrera, and Tupac Shakur, recognizing the literary achievements of people of Color who previously had been absent from the curriculum.

The practice created opportunities for students to develop the academic skills associated with analyzing poetry while accessing poems connected to their lived experiences. Mr. Parsons was able to teach students to identify literary elements and techniques such as figurative language and symbolism in the poems they brought to class. He asked students to highlight at least five words or phrases in the poems that connected to their interests or cultural backgrounds. Asking youth to share how the poems connected to their lives prevented Mr. Parsons and others from making assumptions or relying on stereotypes about how and why youth saw themselves reflected in the poems they chose. The activity supported Mr. Parsons's cultural competence and provided students with more-nuanced understandings of their peers' experiences and perspectives. Moreover, Mr. Parsons extended the lesson to include students' analysis of poems sanctioned in the school curriculum at a level of rigor supportive of student learning and achievement, and their cultural backgrounds, identities, and interests.

Focus on School Culture

The CRE-PD also created opportunities for educators to better understand, and sometimes challenge, their colleagues' stereotypes about culturally and linguistically diverse students in their school communities. Buena Vista High School, for example, has a predominantly White, middle-class, female teaching staff, and a student body comprising wholly Black and Latinx youth. During an early session of the CRE-PD, Tina, a White female educator at the school, shared her response when issues of race came up in an advisory class she taught over the course of 3 years. Tina said she did not see Color and that there was no difference between her and her students. When students wanted to discuss stereotypes about them based on the shade of their skin tone, Tina told them they were all human beings and that skin color didn't matter.

Kevin, a White male teacher at the school, pushed back against Tina's statement, challenging her to take a more critical stance in her interactions with students. He began sharing about a Black male student who many of the teachers knew who had attended Buena Vista High School and was currently a freshman in college. Kevin said the student discussed with him an essay about his negative high school experiences based on stereotypes related to his dark skin. Later, Tina approached Michelle and said that after listening to Kevin's comments, she went back to the students in her advisory group and reminded them of their previous conversation about stereotypes they encountered based on their skin color. Even though she was still uncomfortable talking about race, Tina explained to Michelle that she had spent 3 years as the students' advisory teacher. She felt as if she owed it to them to talk about how she previously had not acknowledged their concerns. She then deliberately asked students to share about their positive and negative experiences based on their skin color. Tina said it was difficult to do so, but that Kevin's comments and her participation in the CRE-PD helped her to see that she couldn't ignore her students' concerns when they said their skin color affected their schooling experiences.

Through their interactions in the CRE-PD, Tina and Kevin became more aware of the importance of talking about issues of race and how they impact ways in which students experience a school's culture. The educators demonstrated a developing sociopolitical consciousness and built upon students' "aware[ness] of society's prejudices and biases," an invisible strength highlighted in Figure 3.2. Further, by sharing the perspectives of a former student, Kevin drew on the young man's invisible strengths, making visible his resiliency and adaptability in navigating identities and relationships, and his interest in sharing his experiences. The practice further supported Tina in looking critically at her own practices while developing cultural competence considerate of the experiences and strengths of the former student who wrote the essay. As a result, Tina created opportunities within the context of the advisory class to talk with students about negative stereotypes they encounter, and how they seek to navigate those stereotypes. When educators have opportunities to share examples of when, how, and why they acknowledge students' lived experiences and negotiate stereotypes of multiple identities, they may support one another in enacting similarly critical practices.

Focus on College and Career Readiness

For some teachers, participating in the CRE-PD provided language and strategies necessary to challenge their own and others' deficit-oriented stereotypes and assumptions about youth. For example, one educator noted:

> The sessions emphasized the importance for us to not come into this environment with limitations. To have high expectations for our students. To come into this community where there are challenges, but a lot of potential and to have high expectations for our students.

Rather than assume that students of Color have only negative experiences as reflected in the deficit-oriented stereotypes in Figure 3.1, culturally relevant educators seek out opportunities to better understand the nuanced experiences of their students. Developing high expectations encouraged teachers to embed students' college-going identities into their interactions, and to draw on students' strengths rather than negative stereotypes of their lived experiences and perspectives. For example, Mr. Michaels, a Black teacher, shared:

> In one of the CRE trainings we talked about how you might say certain things to the kids, not realizing you're lowering their self-esteem. You know we might get frustrated with how they are academically. And we might say, you know, like, "Some of your only options might be working at McDonalds." Not looking at where they are to build up on it. Not looking at the negative in the situation, but kind of looking at what their resilience is and use it as a springboard to help improve them.

Mr. Michaels's ability to reflect on how his frustration with students' academic performance might be "lowering their self-esteem" signals a shift in how he perceived a deficit-oriented future career for the students versus a strengths-based perspective of the students' resilience that he could build upon.

In a focus group interview, a group of teachers at another school discussed how the CRE-PD sessions led the school's English Department to demonstrate their high expectations for students' academic achievement and college readiness by expecting that all students would write their school research papers using MLA guidelines for style. Previously, not all students were held accountable for writing papers in a way that prepared them for the style they likely would need to use as college students. "We explain to the students that this is what is expected of them in college," a teacher explained. Verbalizing expectations that students will attend college and holding them accountable for enacting writing practices expected in college-level courses challenges negative stereotypes that position youth as unable to meet academic expectations in college-level courses.

CONCLUSION

As educators become increasingly aware of deficit-oriented stereotypes and assumptions about youth of Color prevalent in U.S. society, they are better prepared to challenge their own assumptions about the students enrolled in their classrooms and school communities. The examples provided throughout this chapter demonstrate that educators who explicitly address the role that race, ethnicity, and stereotypes play in their interactions with culturally diverse students, particularly when it comes to negative stereotypes and implicit biases, are better prepared to enact culturally relevant practices that support student learning and achievement. To continue to challenge deficit-oriented stereotypes of youth of Color prevalent in today's society, educators must engage in honest conversations, with their colleagues and their students, that reflect youth's lived experiences negotiating such stereotypes.

Furthermore, in specifically examining opportunities to make youth's strengths visible, educators consider how they may enact more-equitable practices in their classrooms and school communities. When educators are able to name the negative assumptions their students encounter, they are better equipped to consider how they might recognize and build on youth's invisible strengths in the areas of curriculum and teaching, school culture, and college readiness. Building on the strengths of students provides opportunities for educators and school leaders to see places of convergence in strengthening their relationships with students, as discussed in Chapter 4.

We recommend that teachers, counselors, principals, and other adults who work with culturally and linguistically diverse youth take up the questions below, independently and with their colleagues, as a step toward making visible the strengths youth bring with them into their classrooms and school communities, and so as to create more culturally relevant and equitable educational opportunities for youth.

QUESTIONS AND ACTIONS FOR INDIVIDUALS AND SMALL GROUPS WITHIN SCHOOL COMMUNITIES

1. Create opportunities to come together with colleagues to talk about some of the stereotypes you hold about your students. Support one another in explicitly addressing the role that race, ethnicity, and stereotypes play in your interactions with students, particularly when it comes to negative stereotypes and implicit biases you may hold and enact toward your Black and Latino male students (this will be discussed in further detail in the next chapter).
2. As you engage in popular media over the course of a week (or another timeframe), make a list of the stereotypes you see enacted around you—toward you or toward others. What do you notice when you look at your list? Are there particular popular media outlets that forefront particular stereotypes? Are there particular cultural or linguistic groups that are stereotyped more often than others?
3. Consider how the curriculum, teaching, school culture, and college and career readiness practices in your own school community reflect your students' invisible strengths or further deficit-oriented stereotypes.

4. View the online videos listed below and make a list of stereotypes and strengths of students portrayed in each video. Consider how you may assist students in negotiating the stereotypes depicted in ways that build on youth's invisible strengths in society and schools.

   a. Hernandez-Saca, D., & Adai, T. (2013). *Dr. Howard on Black students*. United States: Equity Alliance. Retrieved from vimeo.com/66858441

   b. Greenberg, B. (2015). *Gloria Ladson-Billings—Successful teachers of African American children*. United States: Brainwaves Video Anthology. Retrieved from www.youtube.com/watch?v=hmAZjNRmall

CHAPTER 4

Building Productive Teacher–Student Relationships

Constructing New Academic Practices

Inquiry Focus: How may educators develop productive, meaningful relationships with students that reflect similarities and differences in their cultural backgrounds?

Opportunity: Educators connect with and promote success for all students, particularly youth of Color.

But what do I actually do in my classes? Especially when I'm not Black, Latino, or male? They can kinda connect to them in a different way. But, what can I do as well?—Lois, White female teacher

It's also about making a connection too. Once you make the connection you get more respect from the students. Something I love to do is I'm also a track coach. So, one thing I'll do is I'll do a survey; okay who's on a sports team? They'll say track, baseball, basketball, things like that. And then once they come in again, if I know they had a game I'll say, "Oh how was your game yesterday?" you know and they'll tell me. And I'll go visit their games too. Once you break that teacher–student mentality, they're like surprised. They see me at the store down the street. . . . But then we have conversations about what's going on in the school and they feel more comfortable with you, so you break that down. And then they feel more relaxed. And then they will actually do more work and then they'll listen to you even more. It's all about making that connection. You're going to get so much out of them once you make that connection.—Alberto, Latino teacher

In this chapter we share how teachers built upon what they learned in the culturally relevant education professional development to explore their racial identities and examine the development of productive relationships with students. Specifically, we highlight examples of teacher–student relationships and how teachers began to make connections to academic practices. Alberto's and Lois's reflections reveal the opportunities and challenges that teachers encountered as they thought about how they talked about their racial identities and whether they were able to develop a sense of connectedness (or not) with youth of Color, specifically their Black and Latino male students. Some assumptions and tensions also emerged in their statements that highlight the need for further critical reflection. For example, is there an assumption that it will be easier for teachers of Color than for White teachers to connect to students of Color? Even if teachers of Color can connect to students of Color based on similar racial/ethnic experiences, is there an assumption that they will be effective teachers of students of Color (Jackson & Knight-Manuel, 2018)? We recall Brandon's remarks in Chapter 1, where he noted how he thought he knew everything since he grew up as a person of Color in New York City, but the CRE-PD taught him there was more to learn to support his students.

Another tension emerged when it became readily apparent that some White educators, despite their willingness to connect to students, felt that they could not develop relationships with youth of Color because they did not share racial/ethnic and cultural backgrounds. Alberto and Lois invite us to think about how learning in collaboration with one's colleagues increases capacity to develop and/or strengthen the dispositions and skills needed to build meaningful relationships with students of Color to support them academically, socially, culturally, and civically. Specifically, we invited educators to think about the role that a teacher's racial/ethnic backgrounds play in building trusting relationships with students and how teachers can connect to students through an understanding of students' racial/ethnic and cultural backgrounds, interests, and daily lives inside and outside of the classroom (Durden & Truscott, 2013).

In Gloria Ladson-Billings's book, *The Dreamkeepers* (1994), she specifically highlights how both African American and White teachers were identified by parents/families as being successful educators of African American students because they engaged in culturally relevant pedagogies characterized by taking responsibility for educating the whole child. Research has shown the salience of positive teacher–student relationships as a mediating factor in student achievement (Rodríguez, 2008; Stanton-Salazar, 2001; Valenzuela, 1999). For example, positive teacher–student relationships can influence teachers' academic expectations, student engagement in learning, and college outcomes. Moreover, while research shows that girls seem to have closer relationships with their teachers (DiPrete & Buchmann, 2013), Fergus, Noguera, and Martin (2014) argue that successful outcomes for Black and Latino males can be attributed to the relationships that they have with teachers. As Alberto noted in the beginning of the chapter, student engagement and learning increase when youth

> . . . feel more comfortable with you. . . . Then they will actually do more work and then they'll listen to you even more. It's all about making that connection. You're going to get so much out of them once you make that connection.

Narratives about student learning and achievement tend to emphasize only academic outcomes. Culturally relevant educators are also aware that educating the whole child involves affirming students' cultural identities and sociopolitical consciousness, which can occur through the development of meaningful teacher–student relationships inside and outside of the classroom.

EVERYDAY PRACTICES IN CONTEXT

There were no bells signaling the start and end of classes at the high school where Joanne taught secondary English for more than a decade. As a result, it wasn't unusual for Joanne to be finishing up a lesson when students dismissed from another teacher's class would begin walking into the classroom to start the next class period. To avoid the ensuing disruption, Joanne developed a habit of closing the door to her classroom near the end of class and opening it when she was ready to dismiss the current group of students and welcome the next group.

While initially intended as a classroom management strategy, the practice had an unintended consequence: In standing at the door at the end of one class and the beginning of the next, Joanne was able to say goodbye to the students in the class she just dismissed before greeting each of the students scheduled for the next class period. While brief, those daily interactions served as the foundation for relationships Joanne developed with the students she taught over 13 years as a high school English teacher. Specifically, Joanne used the time strategically to demonstrate high expectations for students' academic achievement, learn about their lived experiences in ways that she could incorporate into course curriculum, and raise students' sociopolitical consciousness.

In greeting students at the beginning of each class session, Joanne purposefully encouraged them to spend their time together in a productive way, demonstrating high expectations for their academic achievement. For example, she would greet students by name and share that they were going to love what they were about to do in class that day, remind students to get started on their daily "warm up" assignment, say she was happy to see them, let them know she enjoyed reading an assignment they previously turned in, or ask how the class they just finished had gone. For students who missed a previous class, or did not complete a required assignment, Joanne used the greeting as a way to privately remind them to meet with her after class or to be sure they turned in missing work so it did not negatively impact their grade. If students slowly made their way down the hallway to class, Joanne would call to them to hurry so they made it before she closed the door and they were officially late. If a student appeared upset or did not return Joanne's greeting, she often would stop by the student's desk during the first few minutes of the class period, when students typically responded to daily writing prompts, to check in and make sure the student was okay.

While the practice of greeting students at the start of every class took a few more minutes than just allowing students to enter the room independently, students told Joanne that they appreciated the time she took to talk with them each day and to acknowledge their presence in the class. Opportunities also were created for Joanne to ask students about what they had done the night before, whether they had attended a particular extracurricular activity, or what they planned to do during the upcoming weekend. Joanne then sought to make connections between students' lived experiences and their work in the secondary English classroom. For example, when students entered the classroom holding permission slips for an upcoming marching band fieldtrip, she asked them to share reasons they wanted to attend the trip as part of a lesson on writing a thesis statement in an argumentative essay they were drafting.

Saying goodbye to students at the end of each class session had a similarly powerful impact. First, it created an opportunity for Joanne to demonstrate her high expectations for students' academic achievement by holding every student accountable for participating in the learning that took place in the classroom. As she stood at the door, she required students to hand her written reflections, exit slips, or assignments completed in class before they could leave the room. Joanne found that students were more likely to complete and submit their work when required to hand it directly to her than when she asked them to leave their work in a basket on a table near the door. Students who did not complete assignments were sent back to their desks to do so or asked to write a quick note to Joanne stating what prevented them from completing an assignment. When Joanne was aware that particular students struggled with a lesson, interacting with them as they left the room provided a structure for acknowledging students' need for support. For example, Joanne would note that the day's lesson was a bit hard to follow and that she'd take time to review the main ideas during the next class, or thank students for trying their best during a challenging assignment. In affirming students' efforts, Joanne developed relationships with each of her students by letting them know that she saw them, they mattered to her, and she wanted them to achieve in her class.

Now, more than 16 years after she began greeting students at the door to her classroom, Joanne continues to sustain relationships with students she taught over the years. They communicate over Facebook messenger, text messages, phone calls, and social media platforms to share updates of what is happening in their lives, or to reflect on their schooling experiences. Recently, for example, Joanne was tagged in one Facebook post where a former student noted that a text they read in class 6 years earlier was set to be released as a movie, and in another where a Black male student provided a link to an online essay he wrote describing a conversation he had with Joanne after class. He wrote:

> It's amazing how essential the small moments are. Imagine being back in eleventh grade. Only sixteen, you're seemingly invincible but don't realize all the untapped potential you have at your feet. A teacher approaches you after class, explains to you that they want you to apply to this program for after-school internships, and helps you realize that there are actually other people out there who believe in you. This was my story, and literally five words from my junior year English teacher changed my life . . . "I had you in mind." Now I know that doesn't seem so major, but understand to a young adult who barely believes in himself, it's a game changer. (Longsworth, 2018)

The student explained he applied for the internship program, was chosen to participate, and spent several years as an intern for the organization. He wrote: "I felt powerful, I felt loved, I felt fully capable and ready to challenge the world as a young minority excited to show the world what he was made of. All of this because my teacher basically said she believed in me." While Joanne's relationships with students were fostered across multiple experiences over time, they were built on the foundation of care formed by those daily conversations at the doorway at the beginning and end of each class.

In the sections that follow, we share three areas of inquiry we engaged in with educators in the CRE-PD. Specifically, we consider the essential role care plays in relationship building with students, especially students of Color. An ethos of care is reflected in understanding the qualities of a warm and demanding teacher (Delpit, 2012; Ware, 2006), in foregrounding student voices, and in building from their own existing educational practices. For example, in a focus group interview after their participation in the CRE-PD, five educators from Constitution High School said their previous teaching practices could have been considered culturally relevant, but they were unfamiliar with the tenets of CRE, so did not name their practices in that way. Specifically, the educators noted how the CRE-PD helped make their efforts to improve educational opportunities for their students more conscious and purposeful. We share some of those practices in the inquiry focus sections that follow.

INQUIRY FOCUS #1: REFLECTING ON RELATIONSHIPS WITH TEACHERS

How do educators' reflections about relationships with their own high school teachers influence how they develop relationships with students they teach?

One promising approach for engaging educators in critical reflection about their assumptions of how they can connect to students, especially students of Color, involved asking educators to discuss one of their favorite teachers. We invited teachers to respond to the following questions in a written reflection: What subjects did s/he teach? What qualities did s/he possess? Why do you think that you still remember this teacher?

Across several of the high schools, certain qualities of a culturally relevant caring teacher were clearly evident as educators were eager to share about their favorite teachers. It is important to note that while each educator had different specific reflections, particular characteristics that they valued in a favorite teacher were shared across reflections. Several of the qualities that the teachers in the CRE-PD expressed as important were their teacher's ability to take an interest in them personally, a sense of humor, the disposition to encourage them to be their best self and suggest specific ways to do so, and, in some cases, a shared ethnic identity. For example, one teacher wrote that his

favorite HS teacher was a tall person (6'4") broad shoulders, and stern. He taught Computer Repair and Computer Networking. Qualities that stood out were those that are similar to my father's. He became my mentor, which is one major reason as to why I still remember him. Also, he would push me to take advantage of as many opportunities as I was able to. (Male teacher, Eastern Prep Academy, 2013)

Another educator wrote about Mr. Fareed, who taught electronics. "He was funny, he was understanding, he never yelled, and controlled a class of 30 boys. He set me down the path I am on. Who I am is modeled on who he was to me" (journal response, 2013). Another teacher shared that "no one really stands out other than my Italian teachers. I think I had a strong connection to the class because I am Italian . . . and we went to Italy together" (journal response, 2013).

Many educators noted that their favorite teachers were those who were passionate about their subject matter and who also strived to support the educators to be their best. One educator remembered Ms. Denham, an algebra teacher they had in 6th and 7th grades, writing that Ms. Denham was "energetic, cheerful, strict, lenient, communicative, knowledgeable, passionate, dedicated. She made learning simple. She supported us outside of school. She kept us in mind and made us feel like a part of her life" (journal response, 2013). Similarly, a teacher at Borough Academy wrote that "my favorite teacher in high school was Ms. Kane. She taught English. She had a love for every student. She taught and encouraged them to rise beyond their greatest potential and how to value ourselves in any setting. I will always remember her because she made me become a bold individual." Another educator shared about their favorite teacher, Mr. Thomas, "who was young, cool, and revolutionary. He taught us not to accept the norm and fight for what we believed in. He taught social studies well. He was invested. He cared and he was a mentor" (journal response, 2013). For another educator, Mrs. Anand, a 6th-grade humanities teacher, "came to mind immediately":

> She was patient, nurturing, and extremely dedicated to her students and job. She found creative ways to motivate us to read and write. Once, when I was going through some emotional struggles, she arranged for a parent–teacher conference with my mother. It was then that I realized how much she cared about me.

The characteristics that many of the educators identified in their favorite teachers reflect pedagogical practices rooted in notions of culturally relevant care (Gay, 2010; Jackson, Sealey-Ruiz, & Watson, 2014). They also emphasized pedagogical practices that made the subject matter relevant to their daily lives, and the use of humor was mentioned by educators across several schools. Teachers engaged students in authentic, genuine caring relationships that "set high standards" and "pushed" students to meet them with a "heightened sense of their capacities" (Watson, Sealey-Ruiz, & Jackson, 2016, p. 981). For instance, one educator wrote about Mr. Peters, who taught social studies and was "kind, interesting, self-critical, honest, great listener. I remember this teacher because he allowed me to express my voice and opinion and never judged or criticized. He encouraged me to question things, expand my mind" (journal response, 2013). These educators were able to take risks with their intellectual learning as they knew that their teachers believed in them. Delpit (2012) calls such teachers that taught "successful" African American students "warm demanders." Specifically, having high expectations and scaffolding learning for students undergirded many of the teachers' abilities to build upon and strengthen students' academic identity through engendering high self-esteem and academic excellence.

After reflecting on their experiences with a favorite teacher, we asked educators to consider a teacher they disliked as a high school student. What subject did s/he teach? What qualities did s/he possess? Why do you think that you still remember this teacher? We then engaged in lively discussion, with educators enthusiastically sharing out their responses. Teachers were very expressive and, in some cases, quite agitated when they shared about teachers they didn't like. In their journal responses, educators focused on the low expectations teachers had for them, their lack of connection to the subject matter, and personality traits that they didn't like. For example, one teacher shared how "Ms. H. was moody, forgetful, unorganized, angry. I remember how she would give up on us." In a similar vein, another teacher shared how his math teacher, Mr. A., was "very strict, not supportive and told me I was not going to amount to anything. I would be in jail or drug rehab." In addition to low expectations, teachers who were disliked did not support students in their subject matter. For example, one participant remarked that they "never connected with my math teacher. She made math difficult." Another teacher wrote, "My ninth-grade biology teacher was impatient, unfair, and downright lazy. She used to take smoke breaks in the locker room during class. I'll never forget the time that she picked up my science project display and threw it on the floor while I was presenting, because she thought of it as a mediocre project (it was actually a good project, she didn't understand it)." In the above examples, it is clear that educators recalled years later teachers who had not engaged in culturally relevant pedagogies that emphasized caring relationships, a passion for their subject matter, and the ability to teach and make relevant connections between the students and the subject matter.

This process of critical reflection allowed educators to analyze their experiences of connecting to and learning from their own teachers (or not). Critical reflection can serve as a basis for building relationships with students that emerge from understandings of culturally relevant care. Teacher–student relationships shift from those focused on deficits to those that are humanizing (Paris & Winn, 2013). As Cathy shared:

> I think it was more . . . the majority of what I took away . . . my mindset toward them. So, I think from the first day when we were looking at the statistics [of how male students of Color were not succeeding in their school] and then we all sat in groups and we were talking about personal experiences. I think we did that the first day. It was kind of like as a teacher, we're so focused on ourselves and focused on our lessons that we don't realize that a lot of what we're doing is affecting how they're going to view their education years down the line. So, that first session, when we had to look back on our own high school experiences really made me shift gears for the next day in how I set up their high school experience. So, I really enjoyed that.—Cathy (Interview, High School for Investigation and Inquiry, 2014)

The process of critical reflexivity afforded Cathy the opportunity to become aware of her own life experiences as a high school student, analyze the racial inequities in her students' lives based on school data, and, in turn, think about more relevant practices to engage her students. As we will see in the next inquiry focus, the CRE-PD supported teachers to reflect on racial/ethnic differences between themselves and their students, engage in changing their practices, and connect to their students to better support their learning and achievement.

Autobiographical Reflection—Michelle

I agreed to help chaperone a group of 25 students, 4 young women and 21 young men from a school in the Bronx, to an off-Broadway play in Manhattan called *Schoolgirls*. The principal had agreed to pay for the tickets to the play as she saw a direct connection to the experiences she hoped to provide to students as part of the school's African Club. I had only met the students one time before and felt a little awkward trying to connect to them on the subway train platform. However, one of the other chaperones, Nathalia, who knew many of the students, kept introducing me to them. When we got on the train I was standing next to Lydia, who had identified as South African. I began asking her what she liked about the African Club and why she kept going since it was an hour and a half after school. She shared that although she would say "hi" to some of the other African students in the hallways, she didn't really know them and in the club she was getting to know them. She also talked about how the club was focused on intellectual aspects of Africa, traditions and customs. I then shared that I had been to Cape Town and Johannesburg as part of an educational trip and she seemed quite surprised. However, connecting around places in Africa then led Lydia to begin talking about her family and how she was into nutrition and eating healthy. She shared how her father was previously a bodybuilder and how she wanted to major in a subject that had to do with the body, such as physical education. Building a relationship with Lydia started with a train ride where we discussed places that were familiar to her in her home country and her interests stemming from her father's career as a professional bodybuilder; this gave us common ground to talk about when we met in the African Club. For example, in a recent meeting Lydia brought up the role of fitness in her life and how she now has a choice of summer internships with a celebrity fitness instructor or with the 24-Hour Fitness gym in her city. In adopting a learner stance, culturally relevant educators can build trusting relationships with students by seeking to learn about their life experiences, connecting to shared understandings of their family backgrounds, and building on the interests of students in and outside of school (Milner, 2017).

INQUIRY FOCUS #2: LEARNING FROM MULTIPLE IDENTITIES

How do educators' multiple, intersecting identities support relationship building with youth?

Across their participation in the CRE-PD, both teachers of Color and White teachers discussed developing an awareness of their multiple, intersecting identities through critical reflection. For example, while some teachers of Color noted that they shared the same racial/ethnic background with their students, they also realized that the intersections of their identities may have led to their living vastly different lives than their students. These differences led educators to question how they could connect with their students. In particular, teachers discussed how they sought to provide spaces to listen to student voices.

Culturally relevant care provides opportunities for teachers and students to bring their experiences into their interactions with one another. Such openness can facilitate a process in which students can have their experiences validated (Jackson et al., 2014). As one teacher from the High School for Investigation and Inquiry remarked, "[Allow] them to speak their minds. Let them express themselves." By listening to students' voices, educators found they could demonstrate their care for students through attempts to "recognize the cultures enacted and possessed by young people" (Watson, Sealey-Ruiz, & Jackson, 2016, p. 985). For example, Eric, a Black male teacher, shared:

> Even though most of the teachers in this school kind of share cultural
> and ethnic background of the students that we teach, they still
> have difference life experiences. Just age differences, technological
> differences. And we can impose more beliefs and those things on
> them. So I think now that when we say or try to motivate them using
> our experiences, we tend to look and see how are their experiences
> different from what we experienced growing up. Because although we
> come from the same place, most of us were actually born in different
> countries. So that in itself, you know, is kind of different experience
> . . . so we need to kind of . . . that's where we are and we need to . . .
> at least for me, in culturally relevant education, that's what I think
> about. (Interview, Constitution High School, 2014)

Eric's statement led us to consider the following questions: How can educators begin to reflect upon the identities that they do or do not share with students as well as their existing practices in order to strengthen more positive teacher–student relationships? How can educators build upon those relationships for fruitful teaching and learning experiences within the classroom? In so doing, they can see their experiences as a pedagogical tool to employ in affirming their students' identities and building on the differences and strengths that students bring to school (Jackson & Knight-Manuel, 2018).

INQUIRY FOCUS #3: EXAMINING EXISTING PEDAGOGICAL PRACTICES

How can educators examine and learn from their existing pedagogical practices?

We also had teachers reflect on existing practices that they employed to build relationships with students and how they could further strengthen those relationships. Many of the teachers at Future Tech, who were predominantly White, talked about creating an ethos of care within their own practice. For example, many of the educators discussed the caring, humanizing interactions that they engaged in inside and outside of the classroom. For example, educators discussed how they learned their students' names, spoke to them in the halls and during lunch, and made themselves available to students during class, lunch time, and after school. One teacher mentioned communicating honestly with students: "I share my life experiences with them and make sure that I listen to their needs as well. I invite students to have lunch with me in order to get to know them better. [I'm] approachable, willing to listen, consistent. Reinforce [that I'm] trustworthy. Exchange positive ideas" (journal response, 2014). Another teacher suggested: "Recognize progress instead of passing versus failing. Being honest. Being compassionate . . . being very accessible. Always listen to their issues. Being respectful to them." Another teacher insisted that "I always have high expectations for them. That I will only accept their best. Insist that everyone has an important role to play in the success of the class as a whole (collective success)." Still another teacher spoke about validating the culture and interests of students: "Respecting students as individuals and understand that they have different cultural backgrounds." For example, one educator described a discussion with colleagues, noting:

> We really looked into the whole idea of giving kids a voice and being able to make connections between what's in the classroom and their real world. Because that's when they really start to see the value of what's happening in class. So I think we're really doing more of what I like to call "reality rubs" of what's being done in class and how it

affects you outside. Talking about the whole idea of code-switching. We talk about that a lot. Everyone has a certain way they might talk with their friends or with their neighbors. But when you're in another environment or climate where there's collegiate or professional, you're going to need to be able to switch how you interact with people. So I remember that was one of the things that came out of the [CRE-] PD that we looked at. Like kids have their own sense of ownership of who they are. Sometimes as adults we just negate that, or don't pay attention to it.—Black male teacher (Interview, Civic High School, 2014)

Their humanizing interactions and the practice of starting with students' lives and their experiences allowed educators to understand what was relevant to the students. In this case, the teachers are supporting the students in sustaining the cultural and linguistic competence of their communities, while simultaneously opening up access to mainstream norms of the English language (Henry, 2017; Paris, 2012). Affirming students' linguistic identities and supporting code-switching raise the consciousness of students of Color about the different linguistic repertoires that are needed and the different settings in which they can be used (Gay, 2010).

What became very clear was that some teachers were engaging in practices that supported student learning and achievement while affirming students' identities and cultures. We were encouraged that individual teachers were able to take up some notions of culturally relevant care as part of their work in the CRE-PD. However, many educators needed additional support to connect to the sociopolitical aspect that supported students in understanding inequities within their own lives and society, and to think about ways to change those inequities.

CONNECTING TO CLASSROOMS, SCHOOL CULTURE, AND COLLEGE ACCESS

Educators enacted multiple strategies to develop and strengthen their connections to students across the contexts of curriculum and teaching, school culture, and college readiness and access. These strategies occurred inside and outside of the context of the traditional school day and created spaces where all students, especially male students of Color, were able to experience teaching and learning as relevant to their lives. Looking closely at teachers' efforts demonstrates how they made sense of race and equity and enacted culturally relevant practices. We invite educators and school leaders to consider: How are all teachers supported in considering course curriculum and how it is shared with students in ways that take up race, class, gender, religions, and other dimensions of students' identities and their lives that affect teaching and learning in the classroom?

Focus on Curriculum and Teaching

In seeking to build connections between students' lives and learning, we focused on teachers' curricular and pedagogical practices that utilized both culturally relevant and gender-relevant texts in English classes. Affirming students' cultural identities through the selection of texts and focusing on student voice within the curriculum emerged as strategies that teachers used to connect to youth of Color. One teacher shared how he personally responded when other teachers would question the role of cultural relevance in their curriculum:

> People are like, "Cultural relevance? What does that have to do with anything?!" But it really does play a part in how we're looking at the curriculum. And I'll give you a perfect example. English class, in the beginning of the year, she [a teacher] was going very female-centered. The boys were like, aw they weren't really interested. And when the curriculum was designed, no one was really looking at the mixes, if they were heterogeneous or not. So when we went back and tweaked the curriculum we went back and added a couple pieces of literature that the boys would be into. It was a total[ly] different response. And that's something that came out of this. You know the boys, they want to feel like they can connect to the reading, like *House on Mango Street* . . . or other more female books, they may not tie into it as much as *A Long Walk Home* or *Kite Runner*. So we had to go back and look at that and say okay, these are some things we need to change to get them more engaged . . . and we did that.—Black male teacher (Interview, Civic High School, 2014)

Teachers focused on how students engaged in the curriculum by connecting to and affirming the intersections of some of their identities as raced, classed, gendered, and religious. Curriculum that opened up multilayered biographies of youth of Color provided opportunities to reshape the curriculum and pedagogy in ways that were relevant to students' lived experiences (Henry, 2017). The culturally relevant curriculum was academically rigorous, encouraging students' ability to read and comprehend more complex texts. As Henry (2017) notes, "Pedagogies that are relevant to students are pedagogies in which they can see themselves reflected through the curriculum and in which they can imagine their futures" (p. 10).

Focus on School Culture

Teachers reflected on different institutional structures within the school to examine how these structures supported positive relationships between teachers and students, which, in turn, impacted the culture within the school. Advisories were mainly a place for students to engage in academic as well as nonacademic issues with their advisor and peers. An advisory period was one of the strategies used to build positive teacher–student relationships in at least a quarter of the 40 schools (Klevan & Villavicencio, 2016). At Buena Vista High School, for example, each teacher was responsible for advising a small group of students whom the teacher would stay with from 9th–12th grades. As a result, they were able to nurture meaningful relationships across time. In fact, one of the teachers mentioned that her students see her as a "mom," as she has had them in advisory for 3 years and they have discussed various issues affecting them across that time period. Another teacher discussed how he supported students' leadership skills and interests:

> So last month I actually took them to the high school fair, which is also part of the leadership academy at the New York Times building. And that ended on a Sunday . . . it was a 2-day workshop and ended at the Barclays Center [sports arena] for the high school fair. And they also got the opportunity to go to a basketball game that same day at the Barclays Center, floor seats. So I have pictures of that and that was really great. It was fantastic. First time they'd been to the Barclays Center, first time they'd been to a college game. And they got to see also different colleges there for the college fair and different high schools were there as well. Their eyes were like, opened. They didn't realize that this was out there. And that's what I try and do. I do this every year.

He went on to share:

> Once they experience that, it really opens their eyes. They see it's more than just the academics . . . like I said it's all about a connection. And the more you actually get these students involved in the school community, the more . . . the better I think they'll be academically. And they'll achieve more. And I think they'll actually gain more confidence so they'll be going out to the school and be more leaders of the school. Go out for student council, be a class president, go out and do more things. So they're more apt to actually be open to that and not be so confined to their own spaces.—Latino male teacher (CRE Interviews, Metropolitan High School, 2014)

Relationships cultivated inside and outside of the classroom facilitate student engagement within the school and encourage students to open themselves up to new experiences. Culturally relevant teaching practices support students in viewing knowledge critically and engaging in developing the necessary skills to succeed in life.

Focus on College and Career Readiness

Mentoring is an important strategy in building and strengthening teacher–student relationships that support youth's college readiness and access. About half of the 40 schools that participated in the CRE-PD implemented some kind of formal mentoring program (Klevan & Villavicencio, 2016). Some used traditional one-on-one adult–student mentoring. Other schools introduced peer mentoring whereby 11th- and 12th-grade students mentored 9th- and 10th-graders. While the structure and content of these programs differed across schools, the programs shared an explicit focus on nurturing strong caring relationships

During one focus group interview after the CRE-PD ended, some of the teachers at Civic High School noted two different strategies that were sparked or inspired by their participation in the CRE-PD and that supported the development of supportive relationships between teachers and students. Specifically, one teacher incorporated new information from the PD into his male youth group. Another teacher decided she was going to start working with a small group of five Black and Latino young men. She shared:

> And so I decided these were gonna be my five students. And then talking with teachers, and seeing how they were doing in their class and seeing if they were even speaking about college. You know you had other students that were excited and some of them . . . two of them didn't even take the SAT . . . they were adamant in "I'm not taking the SAT," and they had IEPs. So I'm like, okay. So I reached out to their parents to see what else was going on and see how they were speaking. If the parents were mentioning anything to the student. And then to learn that the parents were like "I don't even know." They wanted him to go to school but to get him excited in terms of wanting and desiring that . . . that next step. What's going to be your next step out of high school? Where do you see yourself in 5 years? Because that's something I always ask my students . . . like you're 18 now, what are you gonna do when you're 22? Where do you see yourself when you're 22 or 23? Because that's like, right around the corner. And they think it's so far away. (Interview, Civic High School, 2014)

She opened up opportunities to create a mentoring structure within her school. Yet, while creating a mentoring structure is important, it is not enough to support productive relationships. Through this mentoring structure the teacher sought to build relationships with her students and support their learning and achievement by focusing on their interests and scaffolding their experiences about their college interests, as seen in the following excerpt:

> I sat down with each one of them, I did a folder, we took, we did a list of what they like. What subject do you really like and why? Do you like art? I had some students who were really into art, like going to see plays. Like I never would have thought that . . . or like music. They're into a lot of outside activities. So within that discussion I say, oh, let's look at some of the colleges. So I give them the booklet, they went home, they looked at it. And I tell them to make their list. Even if you have three schools, your top three schools and then we'll work from there. And explaining to them this is what you need and this is how you do it. And then in the morning having them come to the computer and actually fill out the application. I think that was the hardest part. You know like "oh what does the application look like?" And then they realized for the community college it wasn't even that difficult. So once they got over that fear it was like, "Oh ok it wasn't that bad."
> —Black female teacher (Interview, Civic High School, 2014)

Productive relationships are built through the types of interactions that teachers have with students and how they position themselves in these interactions. The teacher provided hands-on tasks that addressed the students' fears and allowed them to be successful in completing their college applications. Thus, she was able to create a mentoring structure within her school to support students' learning and achievement by focusing on the students and their interests, and scaffolding their experiences to address and build upon their college interests.

CONCLUSION

Building trusting, caring, and authentic relationships with students provides a foundation of connection that not only keeps students engaged in schools, but also supports students in being the best that they can be. These relationships serve as mediators to the academics that teachers want students to excel at in their classrooms. It is important to note that relationships that take into account students' interests outside of the classroom facilitate learning and achievement within the classroom.

**QUESTIONS AND ACTIONS FOR INDIVIDUALS AND
SMALL GROUPS WITHIN SCHOOL COMMUNITIES**

1. Take time to reflect on a teacher you liked and one that you disliked. What qualities stand out for you? How are these qualities connected to the tenets of culturally relevant pedagogy?
2. How might you begin to understand your students' interests and goals? Consider opportunities to talk with students informally about their daily lived experiences both in school and outside of school. What connections might you make between your teaching and students' interests?
3. What schoolwide structures exist, if any, that support educators and students in developing productive relationships with one another? How might structures, such as regularly organized fieldtrips, advisory groups, or other opportunities for educators and students to interact outside of the classroom, be developed? What opportunities exist that could support teachers and students in developing productive relationships as part of the classroom curriculum?

CHAPTER 5

Facilitating Culturally Relevant Peer Interactions

Building on Youth's Relationships with Peers

Inquiry Focus: What practices support educators in learning about and building on youth's relationships with peers to support student learning and engagement in culturally relevant ways?

Opportunity: Strengths-based perspectives of youth's relationships with peers facilitate curriculum and teaching that support academic achievement and engagement for youth of Color.

I'm wondering how many kids think this way and say, I choose my friends. I hope they do, I would love for it. Sometimes I'm like, did you really? The mature kids, maybe. Or the kids who have a very reflective sense of themselves.—Lillian, Black teacher, Washington High School (Fieldnotes, 7/7/2013)

You know there was a time when we looked at kids being in gangs as really negative. We didn't understand the output. But then the idea of kids wanting to be a part of something, to feel validated . . . and have someone to associate with. . . . [You can] come in with the detrimental aspect or instead say like okay this kid is someone who wants to be a part of something, let's try to create some environments here so they can be a part of something but it'll have some positive attributes.—Black male teacher (Interview, 4/8/2014)

The role youth's peers play in one another's schooling experiences, particularly when it comes to preparing to enroll in college, has been well documented by education researchers (Sallee & Tierney, 2007; Stanton-Salazar & Spina, 2005). Yet many of the educators we worked with across the CRE-PD did not initially view youth's peer relationships as culturally relevant resources for supporting students' engagement in school. When we asked educators at Borough Academy, for example, to generate a list of supports for student achievement in their school community, students' peers did not make the list. We were not surprised when educators in other school communities similarly looked past youth's peers when thinking about resources that could expand access to equitable schooling experiences for youth of Color. After all, as Lillian notes in her comment above, it might seem to adults that students enter into relationships with their peers haphazardly, or that only academically successful students are intentional about choosing their friends, while less successful students are not. Moreover, many teachers we have collaborated with over the years told us that, as a classroom management strategy, they intentionally minimize opportunities for youth to interact with their friends. Separating students from their friends often is seen as a way to prevent youth from becoming distracted or talking during instruction.

Yet the practice of limiting students' engagement with peers, particularly those peers they consider friends, directly contradicts our understandings of culturally relevant educational practices. For example, adopting strengths-based perspectives of youth's peer relationships provides an opportunity for educators to acknowledge and build from social relations among students and to bridge the gap between youth's home and schooling experiences (Ladson-Billings, 1995a). Specifically, we argue that educators can support culturally and linguistically diverse students' collective notions of achievement by acknowledging, supporting, and building on their culturally relevant peer interactions, including the ways they: (1) hold high expectations for one another's engagement in school; (2) build from shared cultural experiences to negotiate tensions emerging from the cultural mismatch between home and school; and (3) develop and extend notions of sociopolitical consciousness that challenge structural inequities contributing to the opportunity gap too often experienced by youth of Color.

In this chapter, we discuss challenges educators experienced in reconsidering their assumptions about whether, how, and why youth of Color interact with their peers in productive ways that support their academic achievement and engagement in school. We then turn our attention to the practices we engaged in with educators in our attempt to guide them toward enacting strengths-based perspectives by acknowledging and building from youth's culturally relevant peer interactions. Finally, we examine possibilities for more equitably supporting the academic achievement and school engagement of youth of Color, specifically Black and Latino male students.

EVERYDAY PRACTICES IN CONTEXT

As a high school English teacher in New York City, Joanne often stood in the hallway as students passed from one class to the next. It was when students were on their way back upstairs from lunch, held in the basement cafeteria, that she most often observed friendships that never crossed the threshold of her classroom. Students enrolled in different sections of the classes Joanne taught came together during those moments after the school-wide lunch period. They walked together, carried one another's books, ran after one another, and stood at their lockers talking and laughing. Joanne wondered how she could build from the energy and enthusiasm she saw in youth's interactions with one another to support their engagement and achievement in the English courses she taught. An opportunity came when Joanne organized a fieldtrip to a local college campus for students enrolled across the four sections of 11th-grade English she taught.

As a graded assignment, Joanne asked students to work in small groups to create multimodal digital representations of the campus tour. However, rather than limiting students to working with peers within their English class, she invited youth to form groups across any of the four 11th-grade classes. While more than half of the students formed self-selected groups with peers in the English class they attended, the remaining students chose to work with peers enrolled in other classes. Of those groups, one in par-ticular stood out. The group was made up of three young Black men and two Latino young men: Alex, Jonathan, Ricky, Dexter, and Harrison. Four of the young men were supported by Individualized Education Plans (IEPs) and had experienced uneven success across school assignments and content areas. As participants in a self-selected group, the youth built upon their existing relationships to assign group roles, navigate challenges in completing their work, and effectively complete the project during a 2-week-long unit that included the campus visit. The digital artifact they produced featured photographs and video clips the youth captured during the campus tour, text the young men wrote and added to when editing the images into a nearly 4-minute-long digital artifact, and audio of rap-per Nikki Minaj's song *Moment 4 Life* (Maraj, Graham, Seetharam, & Williams, 2010). Notably, a photograph the young men took and fea-tured in the video shows college students through a chain link fence that stood between the photographer and the campus (see Figure 5.1). The fence could be seen as representing the barriers to college access the youth navigated across their daily lived experiences. Moreover, for young men who often encountered low expectations for their academic achievement, sharing the project with classmates during English class became a moment of academic success from which to build.

The college tour group project built from youth's strengths, such as their interests in music, video editing, photography, and collaborating with peers, thereby creating culturally relevant and sustaining opportunities for them to support one another's engagement in an academic assignment for authentic audiences. With the young men's permission, Joanne shared the group project with colleagues who also taught them, and who expressed

Figure 5.1. Screenshot from Video Used in CRE-PD to Highlight the Perspectives of Youth Explaining What They Gained from Interactions with Peers

surprise by the amount and quality of the work they submitted for the project. The assignment, which tapped into the young men's interest in spending time with one another, is an example of how youth can be supported in interacting with peers in ways that support their collective college-going identities and academic achievement.

We juxtapose youth's interactions with peers during the college tour project with traditional classroom seating charts that seek to bolster classroom management by separating youth from peers they consider friends, school policies that prevent youth from opportunities to interact with peers throughout the school day, and meritocratic institutional structures that position academic success or challenges as individual achievements or failures. We are left with the following question, which guides the discussion in the remainder of this chapter: How may educators learn about and build from youths' relationships with their peers in culturally relevant ways that support students' learning and engagement in school contexts?

INQUIRY FOCUS #1: RECONSIDERING YOUTH'S INTERACTIONS WITH PEERS

What tensions emerge as educators reconsider their perceptions of youth's interactions with peers?

In order to support educators in building from students' relationships with peers in culturally relevant ways supportive of their engagement and achievement in school, we first sought to examine typically held assumptions about youth peer groups. In our experiences as teachers, researchers, and consumers of U.S. popular culture and media, we have encountered an overwhelming number of negative messages about whether, how, and why youth of Color interact with their peers. Over the years, we sought to make sense of these messages, even as we collaborated with youth who actively contradicted them. So when we invited educators to consider opportunities for supporting their students' interactions with peers in ways that facilitated their academic success, we expected tensions to emerge as educators reconsidered their own assumptions. For example, youth peer groups often have been positioned in education research, popular culture, and news media as contributing to negative behaviors such as drug use, antisocial behavior, and a lack of interest in education (Gibson, Gándara, & Koyama, 2004; James, 2012). As we discussed in Chapter 3, educators' assumptions about youth peer groups influence their interactions with youth. For example, when educators perceive negative stereotypes of youth peer groups as representative of their students' experiences, they limit youth's interactions with one another. Further, as we noted at the start of this chapter, the preservice and inservice teachers we have collaborated with over the years in urban, suburban, and rural settings point to challenges associated with classroom management as a reason for limiting youth's interactions with peers, particularly those who are friends. Rather than provide students with the freedom to interact with peers of their own choosing, educators concerned with keeping their students on task told us they prefer to organize student groups themselves during course activities. As we noted in the "Everyday Practices in Context" section earlier in this chapter, however, youth often experience opportunities to interact informally with peers of their choosing in between classes, during their lunch periods, and in the moments before and after school begins. Failing to build from and extend these existing relationships between peers represents a missed opportunity to more fully support students' engagement in school.

In an effort to better understand how educators perceived youth's relationships with peers, we encouraged them to acknowledge those relationships as sites of possibility for supporting students' academic achievement and engagement in school. Specifically, we provided educators with excerpts from interviews we previously conducted with youth who talked with us about the role their peers played in supporting their academic achievement and engagement in school (see Figure 5.2). The quotes served as a starting point for discussions in which educators examined the perspectives of youth and reflected on their own considerations of whether, how, and why youth chose to interact with certain peers. For example, we asked educators to read the quotations and then reflect on and discuss their responses to the following questions: (1) How do these quotes reflect (or not) your ideas about how youth are influenced by their peers? (2) How do you think you were influenced by your peers in high school? (3) Describe how and why you think youth interact with their peers. How might the assumptions you make about these interactions influence your practices with youth? As Lillian's comments at the opening of this chapter indicate, it can be challenging to hear the messages youth send about the important role peers play in their learning experiences, particularly because doing so requires educators to reconsider what could be long-held beliefs. However, the youth's quotes led participants to debate and discuss the emphasis youth place on their relationships with one another. For example, in considering Tamia's comment (in Figure 5.2), Kourtney, a Black teacher at Constitution High School, noted:

> I think she definitely wants friends that are like her and sees how her friends influence who they are. She considers herself to be a positive person, and wants the people surrounding her to also be positive people. (Fieldnotes, 8/7/2013)

In describing Tamia as reflective, Kourtney extended Lillian's consideration of some youth possessing certain qualities—"the mature kids" . . . "the kids who have a very reflective sense of themselves"—as being those who are thoughtful about which peers they choose to interact with.

This positioning of some youth as capable of enacting purposeful relationships with peers was taken up by Amanda, an administrator at Eastern Academy, who noted:

Figure 5.2. Examining Youth Quotations

"You can use me as an example of why you should go to school, because I may have an okay job, I may have a nice car, but I'm breaking my back to do it. Now wouldn't you rather make the same money sitting at a desk, you know, and just using your mind instead of your muscles and breaking your back all day long? I would prefer a desk job, you know?"—William, Latino male

"When I choose my friends, I choose someone that's more like me. They just want to go to school, do what they have to do, and that's it. They don't want to deal with all those other things at night, those negative things, they just want to deal with the positive and that's it."—Tamia, Black female

"Some of my friends, some of my people from when I was like 9 years old . . . he was like he ain't go to college 'cause he can't, 'cause there was certain things he did when he was my age. And I was talking to him. And I don't wanna end up like that. So it took somebody that's my age to let me see what y'all been tryin' to tell me this whole time."—Abraham, Black male (Knight & Marciano, 2013)

Tamia just reminds me of that one . . . there's always one [who] knows what she wants, [is] mature, calm, speaks well. [It's] not about the outside for her. It's her thing she's doing. She knows that. She's just focused. (Fieldnotes, 8/7/2013)

While we were encouraged by the enthusiasm with which educators discussed the youth's statements, we were concerned by Kourtney's, Lillian's, and Amanda's shared belief that only particular youth can engage in meaningful relationships with peers. In noting "there's always one," Amanda positioned the majority of youth as unintentional in choosing whether, how, and why to develop relationships with their peers. Such an assumption reflects negative perceptions about the majority of youth—those who are not the "one"—and removes educators' responsibility for listening to youth's perspectives or developing the cultural competence to see and understand the emphasis youth place on establishing relationships with peers. Moreover, if most youth are perceived by teachers as engaging in peer relationships haphazardly, educators are missing opportunities to build from and extend youth's existing peer relationships in ways that support their academic achievement.

Rolando, a counselor at Career Success, took up our call to consider possibilities for supporting youth in building from one another's cultural experiences to support their engagement in school and future opportunities. In learning from one another's cultural experience, peers upset traditional notions of role models for academic success or college going. For example, after reading Abraham's quotation, Rolando shared:

I see that he's experiencing stuff, seeing some people get into some deep stuff. Because of what they got into or what happened to them, they couldn't get into college. It prevented them from going. I feel like the commonality between all three, they're all role models. Tamia is the more confident one. But they know "I'm not the superstar role model, but based on what I've experienced the path I've taken or the path I will take, look at me and try to do different, choose your own path."

Rolando's noting that none of the three students is "the superstar role model" supported educators in thinking about how all students learn from their interactions with one another, not only those positioned as high achievers. In other words, peers who share the realities of what it's like to "have an ok job" or not wanting "to end up like that" can serve as role models for achievement in school, college, and careers (Knight, Norton, Bentley, & Dixon, 2004). Educators' expectations that every one of their students, rather than only a select few, can contribute to and learn from one another's experiences, provide an example of viewing students' choices to engage with peers from a strengths-based perspective. Such a perspective serves as an important starting point in creating equitable culturally relevant learning opportunities for youth that build from and extend their relationships with peers.

Autobiographical Reflection—Joanne

It didn't take long for me to realize as a new teacher that students who wanted to interact with one another during class would find a way to do so. The index cards I wrote students' names on and strategically placed on desks throughout the classroom as a way to control where students sat were removed and repositioned, or just plain ignored. Requests for students to complete class assignments silently and independently were met with a few minutes of quiet before conversations between students sprang up around the room. My instructions for students to remain seated at their desks were greeted with requests to sharpen pencils, throw a purposely crumpled piece of paper in the trash, or go get a drink of water. I quickly realized that my efforts to control students' actions and words during what was supposed to be the independent work portion of each day's lesson too often positioned me as a minimally effective enforcer of classroom rules, rather than a facilitator of students' growing understandings of course content. So I began talking informally with students to ask whom they tended to work well with. I used class time to tell students that I was in a study group as part of my graduate studies. I explained how my group members supported me in completing assignments on time and keeping me engaged in discussions about what we were learning. I invited students to be intentional in their own engagement with peers inside our course, and asked them to write down the names of students they would work well with, and those they might not. I stressed the importance of all of us working together as a class community toward collective achievement, while using their lists to form collaborative working groups honoring as many students' written preferences as possible. But perhaps most transformative was my own rethinking of why I had privileged silence as an indicator of learning in my classroom. Once I began to consider youth's interactions with peers as supportive of—rather than detrimental to—students' learning, our work together became much more purposeful and enjoyable. That's not to say I didn't continue to experience challenges in supporting some students in remaining engaged throughout the entire class period. But I was no longer working alone. In privileging students' collective, rather than individual, achievement, we created a classroom culture where students supported one another in making sense of course assignments and content, encouraged one another to meet shared goals of academic achievement, and enjoyed one another's company as they did so. Culturally relevant educators are able to build on the strengths of culturally relevant peer relationships by providing multiple learning opportunities to understand the lesson/curriculum, maintaining high expectations, while developing trust and building classroom community (Milner, 2017).

INQUIRY FOCUS #2: ENACTING STRENGTHS-BASED PERSPECTIVES OF YOUTH PEER GROUPS

How does reframing youth's interactions with peers support educators in enacting strengths-based perspectives of youth peer groups?

To support educators in considering possibilities for acknowledging youth's interactions with peers as strengths upon which to build, we asked them to examine videos featuring youth of Color who discussed how their peers supported their academic achievement and engagement in school. Educators told us that watching and discussing the videos supported their growing understandings of how youth may interact with one another in culturally relevant ways. For example, we asked educators to view and discuss a video about the Posse Foundation scholarship program (Andrews, 2007). The video explained how the program works to identify youth of Color from under-resourced urban communities, sending groups of 10 youth to partner colleges together as a group, or Posse. Students who participated as members of a Posse at one of 26 partner college and universities in 2007 had a 90% graduation rate, according to the video. In 2018, the Posse Foundation partnered with 57 institutions of higher education while maintaining a 90% graduation rate (www.possefoundation. org/posse-facts). Educator and founder of the Posse Foundation Deborah Bial said she started the scholarship program after talking with a former high school student she taught who enrolled in college but did not graduate. The young man said he likely would not have dropped out of college if he'd had the support of his posse. In the video, Bial recalled: "We thought, what a great idea. Why not send a posse or a team of kids together to college so they can back each other up?" (Andrews, 2007).

Watching the video led educators who previously had not heard of the Posse Foundation to consider the supportive role youth of Color may play in one another's college-going experiences. We discussed the high expectations youth demonstrated for members of their posse, and how they assisted one another in navigating the new experience of being college students, particularly as students of Color on predominantly White college campuses. During one professional development session, our discussion included the perspectives of an educator who participated as a member of a Posse in college. Taliah, a teacher at Borough Academy, said:

As a Posse alumna, it's real once you're on campus. But the thing they didn't mention [in the video] is they're supporting you before you go [to college]. You develop relationships with your peer group. You talk about race, culture, socioeconomic status. Developing a bond not just on a surface individual peer level but on a deeper, culturally responsive level. And how do you engage in these conversations with people on the campus, not just with your posse but with everyone else? I wish they had highlighted that part [in the video]. (Observation notes, August 2013)

In her comments Taliah highlights the important role explicit conversations "about race, culture, socioeconomic status" played in her preparation for college. Her comments remind us how youth talk with their peers about their experiences navigating stereotypes based on identities such as race, gender, and social status in ways that support their academic achievement and engagement in school. In addition, Taliah's comments assisted educators in thinking through what additional supports were in place for youth receiving Posse scholarships, and then helped them in making connections back to their own students. For example, we discussed whether youth in the schools where educators worked had opportunities to play a supportive role in one another's educational experiences in high school. However, some participants continued to experience difficulty in demonstrating the high expectations of culturally relevant educators who position all of their students as interested in and able to pursue a college degree. Interestingly, it was Taliah, the educator who had benefitted from her own participation as a Posse Foundation scholar, who noted:

I see positive peer relations among what we label the honors students. I know we're trying to stay away from saying only a certain group of students can do this work, but it's natural among those kids, and maybe the middle performing can do that too, without telling them to. But in my [class] where it's the lowest third and students with disabilities, we have to scaffold that. That's great, but they're easily . . . They're not talking about the college-going process. It's not interesting to them.

The comment created an entry point for Michelle to guide the group in rethinking notions of student engagement and to consider whether and how youth experience access to opportunities that could develop their interest in pursuing a college degree. Michelle said:

I want to push back against the idea that it's natural for some people. They learned it somewhere; at home, school, somewhere. When people say these kids aren't involved, what have we taught them that they are capable of doing? We have to scaffold these activities. Some students seem to get it more quickly. At one school, [educators were] concerned that 9th-graders were not involved. We have to look at that. Why aren't they involved, as opposed to [assuming] they're not interested? Reschedule your clubs to take place at lunch [rather than after school when students may not be available]. Start with this notion that it's not really natural for anyone, but has to take place somewhere.

In pointing out structures that facilitate or hinder students' engagement in school, such as clubs students might have an interest in, Michelle led educators to move beyond surface-level perceptions of how and why youth participate in school.

We shared a second video that more explicitly highlighted the perspectives of youth who explained what they gained from interactions with peers, implicitly pointing to culturally relevant tenets of high expectations, cultural competence, and sociopolitical consciousness. Joanne created the video with students enrolled at the Brooklyn, NY, public high school where she taught. The video emerged from a graduate school assignment as Joanne sought to document how youth considered their relationships with peers to be supportive of their academic achievement and engagement in school (Marciano-Watson, 2011; see Figure 5.3). For example, one student noted in the video:

I think parents nag, and so it goes in one ear and out the other. I think we look at teachers and they're just, they're saying what they're supposed to say. Oh you guys have to go to college because you're supposed to go to college. Or I'm encouraging you to go to college because I'm supposed to encourage you to go to college. But it's different when you hear it from a friend.

Figure 5.3. Screenshot from Video Used in CRE-PD to Highlight the Perspectives of Youth Explaining What They Gained from Interactions with Peers

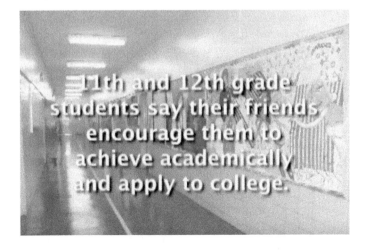

Another student highlighted how the actions of her peers supported her in making positive changes to her own work habits. She said:

> You could look at me and tell that I did not want to do nobody's homework. But I started hanging out with this group of people. It was like, yo, they do their homework, I need to do my homework too. They keep me . . . they keep me on my Ps and Qs.

This student's comments are particularly notable in that they indicate how her interactions with a particular group of peers shifted her previous work habits. While she does not say what led her to start "hanging out with this group of people," her comments supported educators in considering that youth's relationships with peers could be fluid, rather than static, and supportive of more productive and collaborative work habits.

Some educators told us that watching the video helped them to reconsider their assumptions that success in school was a solo endeavor fueled by individual competition. Lillian noted:

> [It] resonated with me, this idea that teachers are saying it because they have to say it. We know as teachers that's not true, but they don't see that. [It] just reinforces why helping them in helping each other in groups is so important.

Yet even after viewing the video, some educators continued to position limited numbers of students as currently experiencing academic achievement with the support of their peers. For example, Rolando noted, "They seem like the driving force for success to college-going culture. If we can start with a small group. You guys set the tone, the example. It sets off like wildfire." While we agree that piloting work with small groups of students can be a fruitful starting point, we encourage educators to further consider all youth as capable of enacting culturally relevant peer interactions, and to design opportunities to scaffold youth into those experiences.

Moreover, we found that even as educators began to view youth's relationships with their peers as productive, they sometimes experienced challenges in positioning themselves as playing a central role in supporting those relationships. While we had hoped that educators would consider how they could support the development of culturally relevant peer interactions in their own teaching, that was often not the case. For example, educators reflected on their own productive experiences with peers in school and often shared that those relationships were developed in the context of after-school extracurricular activities. Kourtney, for example, noted:

> One way for our students to create positive friendships is to have a variety of extracurriculars. As I look back on my own, I think the

extracurricular activities made a big difference, the friends, made my college application look a lot better. Those things outside the school are really, really helpful. I see some kids join a club because their friend did it, but they are still learning something.

We agree that extracurricular activities, where youth often collaborate with peers to achieve a common goal, are one way to support youth's culturally relevant peer interactions. However, consigning the work of developing youth's relationships with peers to the context of extracurricular activities creates inequitable opportunities for youth. Specifically, youth who are unable to participate due to logistical reasons, or who do not have access to extracurricular activities that align with their interests, experience a lack of opportunity. We therefore argue it is necessary for educators to create opportunities for youth to build from and extend relationships with peers across classroom contexts. In the remainder of this chapter, we share insights gained when educators sought to enact more-equitable practices for supporting youth's culturally relevant peer interactions through the creation of institutional structures built into the school day.

INQUIRY FOCUS #3: FACILITATING YOUTH'S CULTURALLY RELEVANT PEER INTERACTIONS

What opportunities exist for educators to facilitate youth's culturally relevant peer interactions while creating more-equitable schooling structures?

Reconsidering youth's relationships with peers provided a fruitful starting point for educators to consider actions they could take in their school communities to create more-equitable educational opportunities for youth of Color. We found that several educators chose to focus their efforts specifically on Black and Latino male students who had experienced academic and/or social challenges at school. Dominic, an administrator at the High School for Career Advancement, described one such initiative after we invited educators to share an action they took in their school communities as a result of participating in the CRE-PD. Dominic shared:

[We have a] group of about 10 boys in our school who were constantly being suspended for play fighting. We went through all of the disciplinary protocols, sat down and said, this isn't working. We can't keep suspending them over and over again. We pulled out one of our deans from lunch and made a male-dominant group. We

took those 10 boys, [they] meet . . . during lunch in two groups. They
arranged themselves. Initially, [they were] not happy to be pulled
out of lunch, their time to act out and be their kind of boys. One of
the parts of the process was they had to submit a daily tracker sheet.
There was a point where they started to rely on each other—go get
this signed, come to me, so and so forgot, but don't worry, he's getting
it signed. In groups, they weren't really doing it before, but they
started to do it. It really does take them being put in a position where
they have to do it. They would encourage each other positively. The
suspension rate really did go down toward the end of the year. Some
of the students were no longer required to go, said we don't need it
anymore. But some of them wanted somewhere to talk to each other
about things. So we're actually going to be doing two groups next year
to cover students, and try female empowerment teams (Observation
notes, 8/7/2013).

It is important to note that a dean, a person of leadership in the school,
thought the program was important enough to want to be a part of it.
Although it's not clear what Dominic means, he notes the youth's lunch time
was when they would "act out and be their kind of boys." In creating consistent opportunities for the young men to support one another, Dominic and
his colleagues offered possibilities for youth to succeed when they received
scaffolded support. The students worked collaboratively to make sure they
completed and submitted the tracking sheets, which required them to obtain
the signatures of their teachers, who indicated how students performed in
class that day. In noting, "There was a point where they started to rely on
each other," Dominic highlights how the youth's understanding of ways
they could support their collective success emerged over time. The consistency involved in the initiative, where students met multiple times per week
over the course of the academic year, appears to be an important aspect of
the group's success.

The level of consistency Dominic noted in his efforts was more difficult
for educators in other schools to attain. Ronald, for example, told us about
an activity that took place in an advisory course at Collaboration Central
High School. Advisory courses were implemented in many of the schools as
a means for educators and students to develop supportive relationships by
talking about issues not typically associated with content-area curriculum.
In the advisory course Ronald discussed, 9th-grade students were asked to
participate in an activity titled "more to me than what you see." In a written
response, Ronald described the activity, noting that students were asked to
identify a fact about themselves they were proud of, and then to share that
fact with the rest of the class. The activity created an opportunity for youth
to discuss their identities. However, the advisory sessions were held only

once a month, making it less clear whether the conversations that began in an advisory session extended beyond that particular session. Moreover, the monthly advisory sessions took place during the time students otherwise would have participated in their physical education class. Ronald noted that a challenge to the advisory session was "the willingness of students to forego their gym period" (written response, 2/7/2013). The positioning of the advisory course in opposition to the physical education course mistakenly could indicate a lack of interest in the advisory course. Moreover, the long period of time between the monthly advisory sessions created additional challenges in developing consistency and purpose.

Another educator, D'Angelo, shared a different action taken in his school community in an attempt to support the interactions of Black and Latino male students. He explained:

> At our school, we have lunch clubs during lunch. Every teacher has a lunch duty. The teacher can pick a week they want to [host a club], put out a list, they give us options and we can go from there. People are still a little hesitant, but we have 30 something clubs, all different things during lunch.

The clubs took place during students' lunch periods in various spaces throughout the school building. Students were still able to eat lunch but also could choose to participate in a club that was of interest to them. Since youth could choose which clubs, if any, to participate in, rather than being assigned to a particular club, they could attend with the peers of their choice. Although teachers chose which weeks they wanted to offer particular clubs to students, the fact that the clubs met during lunch provided some consistency for students who sought to interact with peers outside of the lunch room. Moreover, the structure of holding the clubs during lunch, when all students were present and available to attend, provided equitable access to participation in a way that after-school clubs do not.

CONNECTING TO CLASSROOMS, SCHOOL CULTURE, AND COLLEGE ACCESS

In addition to the examples provided above, we see additional opportunities for educators to extend their support of youth's culturally relevant peer interactions. When educators build from such strengths-based perspectives of youth's relationships with peers, they may enact curriculum and instruction that support academic achievement and engagement for youth of Color. In addition, creating an overall school culture that values and builds from youth's cultural background and experiences provides more-equitable learning opportunities, including college and career readiness, for all students, particularly Black and Latinx youth.

Focus on Curriculum and Teaching

We are particularly encouraged by educators' attempts to support youth's culturally relevant peer interactions through the implementation of advisory sessions and lunch clubs or meetings, as they represent "discourses of possibility," or "the ways in which teachers attempt to think critically about racial identity and power and become involved in social change" (McDonough, 2009, p. 528). Additional opportunities exist for educators to facilitate youth's interactions with peers in productive ways during content-area classes. The *Common Core State Standards for English Language Arts & Literacy in History/Social Studies, Science & Technical Subjects* (National Governors Association Center for Best Practices, Council of Chief State School Officers, 2010) call for students to "work with peers to promote civil, democratic discussions and decision-making" and to "initiate and participate effectively in a range of collaborative discussions." In a written reflection at the conclusion of one professional development session, Lillian, whose comments opened this chapter, wrote, "Peers working together can be/is a really powerful thing!" (8/7/2013).

The video project described in the "Everyday Practices in Context" section of this chapter provided one example of how youth might be supported in enacting culturally relevant peer interactions in the context of course curriculum. Research projects that call upon students to enact Youth Participatory Action Research (YPAR) provide another. YPAR projects create opportunities for youth to examine issues relevant to their lives, such as educational opportunities available in their school communities, while collaborating with peers in ways that develop their academic skills (see Caraballo, Lozenski, Lyiscott, & Morrell, 2017; Warren & Marciano, 2018). To support educators in how they might utilize curriculum and teaching to facilitate youth's interactions with peers, we suggest a review of course assignments and activities. Examining whether, how, and why (or why not) youth are provided with opportunities to work collaboratively toward collective notions of academic achievement can shed light on the challenges and successes educators encounter in connecting this work to curriculum and teaching.

Focus on School Culture

Educators' attempts to alter their school's culture to more actively support opportunities for Black and Latino male students to collaborate with peers hold great promise. As Harper and associates (2014) found in their study of Black and Latino young men in New York City, youth participants chose to spend time in their schools well after dismissal as a way to socialize with peers in a "safe place" (p. 22). The authors noted that "they were not always there for club meetings or rehearsals, but were simply talking and joking, sometimes doing homework" (p. 20). A school culture that leads Black and Latinx youth to choose to be present when they are not required to be is a school culture reflective of educators' culturally relevant practices.

More-structured opportunities exist to further support educators in developing and sustaining a school culture that sees strengths in and builds from youth's relationships with their peers. For example, we have worked with teams of youth in multiple school communities who enacted YPAR projects to examine issues of educational inequities in their school communities. Youth in the U.S. midwest, for example, worked in small-group YPAR teams as part of a community-based effort to understand how high school students experienced access to educational opportunity. The groups comprised youth who attended different public and private schools in the same geographic region and who collaborated to examine how their schooling experiences differed. One group, for instance, interviewed school administrators, teachers, and students to better understand systems of support available to students attending different high schools in the region. The youth learned that while administrators thought students had access to guidance counselors, teachers, and interventionists, students themselves were unaware such supports existed. During a community forum, youth shared findings of their research and recommended new policies be enacted to make students more aware of the supports they could access (Warren & Marciano, 2018). This example demonstrated how YPAR projects position youth as generators of knowledge about topics of interest to them, while contributing to a school culture where youth are positioned as capable of working collaboratively to actively address issues of educational inequities they perceive and experience in their communities.

Focus on College and Career Readiness

Facilitating opportunities for current high school students to talk with former high school students who are enrolled in college supports youth in learning about peers' experiences without interference from educators. In a focus group interview at the end of her participation in the CRE-PD, Jillian described bulletin boards throughout her school community that featured school alumni. She recalled:

> Former graduates who are in college, they came back, they were interviewed. So if we could have more of that and have more awareness of that, yeah, so that our former graduates love to come back and say thank you and visit the teachers and speak to the students. (Focus group, Winter 2013)

When culturally and linguistically diverse youth share insights into their experiences attending predominantly White institutions and the successes and challenges they encountered, opportunities are created for students to learn from peers. Additional opportunities exist for high school students to visit colleges where school alumni are enrolled, and to interact with them while on campus. Alumni may be able to discuss what aspects of their high school experiences prepared them for college, and provide advice for current high school students about actions they might take to support their college-going experiences.

We further encourage educators to consider opportunities for inviting recent alumni back to their schools to participate in career fairs to expose students to additional postsecondary pathways they might be interested in pursuing. For example, alumni who remain close in age to current students and who have chosen to pursue careers as electricians, plumbers, carpenters, visual artists, musicians, or other opportunities that may not require a traditional college degree could talk with students about their credentials, work experiences, or pathways toward job prospects. Providing students with opportunities to learn from recent graduates serves to broaden youth's exposure to information about careers they eventually may seek to pursue.

CONCLUSION

Across our efforts to guide educators in examining their assumptions about whether, how, and why Black and Latinx students interact with peers, several successes and tensions emerged. For example, when we first invited educators to think about culturally relevant peer interactions, they often considered students who purposefully interacted with peers as the exception, and those who performed well academically often were perceived as capable of interacting with peers in productive ways. However, our use of several videos that showed students who discussed collaborating with peers as beneficial to their schooling experiences created opportunities for teachers to consider whether their curriculum, instruction, and classroom management practices assumed that *all* students could work collaboratively with peers in productive ways. In their action plans, educators discussed and developed opportunities for youth to interact with peers in purposeful ways. We recommend that educators take up the questions on the following page to consider their own ideas about youth's interactions with peers, as they seek to create more-equitable learning opportunities for students.

**QUESTIONS AND ACTIONS FOR INDIVIDUALS AND
SMALL GROUPS WITHIN SCHOOL COMMUNITIES**

1. Take time to talk with culturally and linguistically diverse students who experience varying levels of success and engagement in school. Ask them to explain when, how, and why they provide and/or gain support from their peers when they experience challenges inside and outside of school. Ask students how you might create opportunities for students to provide and/or gain similar kinds of support throughout the school day.

2. Conduct an evaluation of your course curriculum, teaching practices, and classroom management policies. How often, if at all, are students of Color expected to collaborate with peers to achieve collective goals? How might your classroom management policies facilitate or hinder students' opportunities to collaborate with peers of their own choosing in purposeful ways?

3. View the online video Joanne created with her students (www.youtube.com/watch?v=X-ErPJ6fbx4). Then, write a written reflection before talking with your colleagues about what you learned from listening to the students' perspectives. Watch the video with your students as a way to begin a conversation about how their peers support their engagement in school.

CHAPTER 6

College Talk

Challenging Racial Assumptions and Inequities

Inquiry Focus: How do culturally relevant educators engage in college talk with youth to strategically and purposefully support educational opportunities for Black and Latinx youth?

Opportunity: Educators support Black and Latinx students in navigating barriers to their educational opportunity, college enrollment, and future careers.

I had a conversation with one of our students about how he probably maybe shouldn't go to [a local community college]. He probably should apply to a drama academy because he really is that talented. And it was kind of like oh I don't know if I'm supposed to be saying . . . go to a drama academy. It's worth your money I guess if this is what you're actually going to be doing. . . . He doesn't like school. But he likes acting.—Martine (High School for Investigation and Inquiry, 10/21/13)

I really think it's rewording and rethinking what we say to kids. I think sometimes because the kids are not performing academically or socially where we want them to be, we kinda shut down and we kinda get the attitude that someone else will deal with it. I think now people realize that this area of the school is a part of the problem. And the things you say to a kid can make or break them.—Andrew (Focus group interview, 5/23/14)

In their statements above, Martine and Andrew highlight tensions that emerged as we encouraged educators to engage in college talk with youth: conversations about whether, how, and why youth could engage in processes related to preparing for, applying to, and/or enrolling in college (McClafferty, McDonough, & Nunez, 2002). At a time when high schools across the nation continue to be called upon to prepare students to meet standards for college and career readiness (National Governors Association

Center for Best Practices & Council of Chief State School Officers, 2010), youth of Color are still graduating from high school and enrolling in college at disproportionate rates (U.S. Department of Education Office of Civil Rights, 2016). Educators must engage in purposeful and culturally relevant college talk as an important component of a culturally relevant schoolwide college-going culture (Knight & Marciano, 2013) to support youth of Color in preparing for college and careers. Such a culture emphasizes a collective responsibility among school personnel for sharing information and supporting students' college access and pursuit of future career goals, rather than relying on guidance counselors as the traditional gatekeepers of information about whether, how, and why youth may pursue a college degree. Culturally relevant college talk is particularly important in under-resourced schools where youth of Color, including those seeking to be the first in their families to attend college, encounter limited access to guidance counselors, creating barriers to college access (Farmer-Hinton & McCullough, 2008; Liou, Antrop-González, & Cooper, 2009; Martinez, 2014).

Even as it has been well documented that the messages educators send youth about their college readiness and access play an important role in youth's college-going decisionmaking processes, teachers and administrators repeatedly tell us that they experience challenges in deciding what information about college and careers, if any, to share with students. For example, students ask questions about which colleges they should consider attending, where colleges are located, and how much it costs to attend college. Additional questions include which colleges offer opportunities to explore particular careers and interests, whether youth are strong candidates for admission, and considerations of differences between public and private colleges and those serving predominantly White students versus students of Color. These questions often lead educators to raise questions of their own. We return to Martine's statement at the opening of this chapter as an example. In noting, "And it was kind of like oh I don't know if I'm supposed to be saying . . . go to a drama academy," Martine highlights a tension educators grapple with as they decide whether it is within their role to share information about specific colleges and careers students might pursue.

For teachers who have not participated in professional development that positions them as "experts" knowledgeable about all aspects of the college application process, or postsecondary certificate programs required for some careers, it can be difficult to recognize the important role of conversations with youth in helping students navigate college-going processes as they consider future careers, particularly for students who may be undocumented. However, research highlights the key role teachers' comments play in sharing information about navigating the college application process with students (McKillip, Godfrey, & Rawls, 2012). "College talk," as it is referred to in educational research literature, is an essential component of a school's college-going culture (McClafferty et al., 2002, p. 11), creating entry points for students to ask questions, share information, and gain multiple perspectives about college and careers.

A number of research studies have analyzed the role of college talk in supporting the college readiness and access of youth, particularly first-generation college applicants (Bryan, Farmer-Hinton, Rawls, & Woods, 2017; McKillip et al., 2012). Specifically, McClafferty et al. (2002) identify college talk as the first of nine "Principles of a College Going Culture" in schools, defining its role in developing a schoolwide college-going culture in the following way:

> A college culture requires clear, ongoing communications with students about what it takes to get to college, so that they understand what is required and expected of them if they want to stay on a college path. Faculty and administrators share their own experiences and discover their own assumptions about their roles in preparing students for college. Through this College Talk, a college culture becomes clearer and the college preparation process becomes more effective. (p. 10)

In this chapter, we enact an inquiry approach to name and understand the successes and challenges educators experienced in reflecting on and enacting college talk with youth of Color in their school communities. We provide examples of college talk that were successful because they were purposeful and built from youth's lived experiences and perspectives. We furthermore draw connections between educators' considerations of college talk in relation to formal and informal school structures that facilitate and/or hinder youth's access to such conversations.

EVERYDAY PRACTICES IN CONTEXT

As a senior in high school, Anna knew she wanted to go to college. She was a student in the 11th-grade English class Joanne taught the prior academic year at a public high school in Brooklyn, NY, and a participant in a research study Joanne conducted to better understand youth's college-going literacy practices (Marciano, 2017; Marciano & Watson, 2017). Anna told Joanne the college application process was new to her; her parents moved to New York from Puerto Rico and had not attended college. While Anna's parents supported her aspiration to attend college, they wanted her to choose a college close to home so she could continue to live with them and commute to campus. So, when Mrs. Easley, a teacher Anna considered a mentor, arranged a campus visit to a selective, local, private, and predominantly White college a mile from the public high school she attended, Anna was thrilled. Not only was the college close to home, but Anna recalled Mrs. Easley telling her she was a strong applicant even considering the college's competitive admissions process. Minutes after arriving on campus, however, Anna's excitement turned to discomfort and her confidence turned to doubt.

> I walked into [campus] and I saw no African Americans or Latinos there. . . . It shocks me. It makes me feel like, if it's like this wouldn't it be a waste of time putting in an application? Should I lie on it and say I'm Caucasian, or Chinese? (Interview, 6/28/2013)

Anna was left to independently negotiate the disconnect she experienced between Mrs. Easley's college talk positioning her as a potential student at the college, and the reality that she did not see anyone who looked like her while visiting the campus. Anna did not mention whether she talked with Mrs. Easley about not seeing any Latinx students during the campus tour and, despite her discomfort, she applied for admission to the college. Her application was denied.

When Anna was admitted to a local community college a few weeks later, Mrs. Easley discouraged Anna from attending, noting that the school was not selective. Anna followed Mrs. Easley's advice and did not enroll. Anna shared, "I am disappointed. 'Cause I had it like planned out. And sometimes, like when everyone's like oh gosh I can't wait for college in the fall and everything and I start to feel like left out (interview, 6/28/13). Joanne's interview with Anna took place a few days after Anna was recognized as one of the top 10 students in her class during her high school graduation ceremony. After graduation, Anna was left to navigate the mixed messages of academic success with her choice not to enroll in college. Anna eventually enrolled in the community college the following spring semester.

We do not share the example above to disagree with the advice Mrs. Easley provided to Anna in her college talk. In fact, in her college talk and facilitation of Anna's campus tour, Mrs. Easley demonstrated high expectations for Anna's college-going future. However, Anna's decision to follow Mrs. Easley's advice not to enroll in the community college highlights the powerful role educators may play in influencing youth's choices as they navigate decisions about whether and where to attend college. These conversations are particularly important at a time when educators nationwide continue to be called upon to support students in becoming college and career ready by meeting academic standards across multiple content areas. (Conley, 2012). As noted in Chapter 1, only two of the 28 schools we collaborated with in the CRE-PD explicitly focused their school purpose on preparing students for careers, and all of the schools sought to prepare students to attend college. To support college—and future career—readiness, we argue that educators must play a strategic role in equitably engaging in college talk with students in culturally relevant ways that build from youth's lived experiences, perspectives, and future-oriented, college-going identities. Mrs. Easley demonstrated high expectations for Anna's candidacy as an applicant to the local, selective private college and demonstrated cultural competence in honoring her family's desire that she attend college close to home. However, had Mrs. Easley been more aware of the disconnect Anna experienced while visiting the college campus, she might have assisted Anna in navigating those feelings in ways that supported her cultural identity. For example, Mrs. Easley might have guided Anna in contacting the college admissions office to ask whether a Latinx student organization existed on campus, or whether school officials could put her in touch with Latinx students currently enrolled in the school. Anna might have gained new insight into whether or how her cultural and linguistic identities might be sustained (Paris & Alim, 2017) if she enrolled as a student on campus. In addition, Mrs. Easley might have guided Anna to apply to local colleges offering strong programs and with a larger Latinx student population than the campus she and Anna visited.

In the remainder of this chapter, we provide insights gained from our work with educators as they reflected on and examined instances where they engaged in college talk with students. Specifically, we share what we learned from encouraging educators to consider how they might extend their college talk with youth in strategic and equitable ways reflective of a schoolwide, culturally relevant college-going culture (Knight-Manuel et al., 2016). We ask: How do culturally relevant educators engage in college talk with youth to strategically and purposefully support educational and future career opportunities for youth of Color?

INQUIRY FOCUS #1: EXAMINING COLLEGE TALK

How do educators examine opportunities and challenges they experience in enacting college talk?

Two distinct understandings emerged from our work with educators as they considered their enactments of college talk with youth of Color in their school communities. First, we learned that educators often talked broadly with students about preparing for and attending college. Second, we learned that educators' college talk often placed responsibility for learning about and preparing for college upon students as individuals. Discussing the tenets of culturally relevant education with educators created new opportunities for considering the benefits of sharing, in their college talk, specific, rather than broad, information that built upon students' experiences and perspectives. Moreover, we supported educators in extending their sociopolitical consciousness by highlighting the role institutional structures play in facilitating and/or hindering educators' purposeful college talk with youth. Such understandings are important in that they may assist educators in realizing that some youth may not see themselves as college-bound because of the deficit-oriented messages they have received throughout their schooling experiences (Knight & Marciano, 2013). Educators who understand the structural inequities that contribute to students' limited achievement in school, such as a lack of access to a rigorous curriculum that builds from youth's cultural backgrounds, may support youth in gaining access to experiences that could assist them in preparing for and applying to college.

We learned the lessons above as we built upon educators' perspectives in ways that acknowledged and extended their existing college talk practices. For example, we asked educators in one of their first encounters with us to share a recent conversation they had with a student of Color about college. Those initial conversations were often enthusiastic, with educators stating they were confident they were talking with culturally and linguistically diverse youth about college. For example, at Buena Vista High School we asked a group of educators to informally share on a scale of 1 to 4 how they thought their school community was performing when it came to college talk with students of Color. We explained that 4 meant they were doing very well, and 1 that they were not.

> *Michelle:* I just want to show by raise of hands, how many of you think Buena Vista is at a 4 for college talk?
> *Jessica:* I have a mixed opinion for it.
> *Michelle:* Ok, in between 3 and 4. How many of you had 3s? . . . So there definitely seems to be some consensus in this room that you're between a 3 and a 4. Do you want to say more about maybe why you're not a 4 yet?
> *Ava:* I feel like we are in ways. We have the evidence. We have the routine, we have the work, we model it. Our supervisors are modeling it for us. We're modeling for the students. So I believe we're doing a little þit of both [3 and 4].

Ava noted that messages about college are evident in educators' "routines," "work," and through "modeling." However, the "evidence" she referred to was vague. We wondered specifically how teachers, counselors, administrators, and school staff shared messages with students about whether, how, and why they can and/or should consider attending college.

Later in the same large-group discussion, Julia shared:

> *Julia:* My only concern with 4 is because sometimes we're spreading a message, you think you're saying something, but it doesn't necessarily mean that the kids get it or that they understand.
> *Michelle:* Ok so maybe what is shared is not necessarily what is learned.

The act of positioning students as responsible for internalizing the messages educators shared about college was common across multiple school communities we worked with. For example, we heard educators talk about students who just didn't "get it" or "understand" the college talk messages educators delivered. However, we encouraged educators to enact strengths-based perspectives of youth by considering the responsibility educators bear for reflecting on and reframing their talk with youth, rather than assuming that students are not interested in learning about how they might increase their college readiness and access. For example, Julia's comments remind us of our work with educators at Constitution High School and the High School for Investigation and Inquiry, who similarly positioned the responsibility for understanding messages teachers sent about college readiness and access on students (Knight-Manuel et al., 2016). Supporting educators in considering culturally relevant practices requires us to push back against assumptions that youth alone are responsible for making sure they "get" the messages educators share in their college talk.

We heard responses that similarly positioned youth as singularly responsible for embracing messages shared through college talk with educators at the High School for Investigation and Inquiry a few months earlier. We asked participants to discuss their written reflections about a recent conversation with a Black and/or Latino male student(s) about college. We purposefully asked educators to write their reflections before discussing their ideas with the whole group, as a way to encourage them to talk about specifics, rather than vague generalizations about college talk they engaged in with youth. The following discussion took place about what they wrote:

> *Michelle:* What kinds of conversations are going on in the building
>   with students around college going? What are they hearing?
> *Patricia:* That they're going.
> *Michelle:* Ok, that's the expectation, that they're going.
> *Patricia:* Yes. Like I think, I don't know, I kind of . . . you're expected
>   to graduate. . . . It's an expectation. The rest of the world, it's
>   expected to graduate high school. Or that you're going to go to
>   college. You're going. So I think that that's, I don't know, that's
>   the tone that I set in my room. They almost don't have a choice.
>   Whether it's college or if it's you know . . . something where they're
>   going to be able to find a path to make a living and have a life,
>   enjoy the things that come with being self-sufficient.

Patricia's reflection shares the broad generalizations, rather than specific examples, we noted in the messages educators sent in their college talk with students. For example, Patricia noted that students encounter the expectation that "they're going" to college, but later added to that statement by saying, "Whether it's college or if it's you know . . . something where they're going to be able to find a path to make a living . . ." Without specifying what that "something" might be, Patricia provides an example of how students were positioned as responsible for meeting the broad expectation that they will graduate from high school and attend college or have to figure out how to "find" their own "path" independently. In addition, we found that educators often positioned youth whom they did not perceive as ready to take on the academic rigors of college curriculum as "career ready." However, it was not clear whether educators in many schools, beyond the two schools focused on career readiness, had a clear understanding of what careers were available to students upon graduating from high school. Moreover, an increasing number of jobs require workers to have some form of postsecondary education (Lumina Foundation, 2018). Educators who are aware of the types of certificates and educational credentials that might be needed to advance in particular careers could support students in understanding how to pursue those careers.

While we sometimes were concerned by what we learned about educators' experiences enacting college talk with students, we gained deeper understanding into their perspectives in ways that influenced our continued work with them. For example, we led participants to begin considering how their own educational experiences influenced their college talk with youth, before providing opportunities for examining how culturally relevant educational approaches could assist them in enacting more productive college talk with youth of Color that built upon youth's strengths to support their academic achievement, college readiness, and college access. We share examples of how this work was taken up by educators in the sections that follow.

INQUIRY FOCUS #2: ENACTING CULTURALLY RELEVANT COLLEGE TALK

> How do CRE practices support educators in enacting more purposeful college talk with Black and Latinx youth?

In seeking to support educators in enacting purposeful college talk supportive of the college readiness and access of culturally and linguistically diverse students, we found it necessary to guide participants in considering how the tenets of culturally relevant education could provide indicators for assessing their conversations with youth (see Appendix B). As we discussed in Chapter 1, educators initially had different understandings of what was meant by the three tenets of culturally relevant education: academic achievement, cultural competence, and sociopolitical consciousness (Ladson-Billings, 1995b). These tenets are particularly important to address as they assist educators and students in considering whether youth will see their cultural identities reflected in the student body, benefit from programs seeking to retain students of Color on campus, and provide supports for first-generation college students, such as advising and tutoring. Therefore, we found it necessary to explicitly discuss with educators how their practices reflected these tenets, and to provide opportunities for building upon existing practices and envisioning and enacting new practices to support students' access to information about colleges they might attend and careers they might want to pursue.

Cultural Competence

As we noted in Chapter 2, educators must reflect on their own identities and cultural experiences in order to enact culturally relevant educational practices with youth. Yet we found that many educators were not considering how their own experiences in college influenced the content of their college talk with youth. For example, Allison noted in a written reflection about a time she engaged in college talk:

> As two students [Michael and Joseph] were filling out applications to colleges that were upstate, I commended them for applying to those schools and told them how going to school outside of the city [New York] would be a very rewarding experience—from being forced to get to know classmates and becoming engaged in college activities and groups to being exposed to people from different backgrounds. I shared a little about the great experience I had going away. They shared that their parents were hesitant about letting them go to a school far away and I shared that my relationship with my parents actually improved because I went away. (College-going conversations handout, Allison, High School for Investigation and Inquiry, Winter 2013)

In her comments to Michael and Joseph, Allison makes an assumption, based on her own experiences, that they, too, would have a "very rewarding experience" leaving their community to attend a college outside of New York City. Moreover, Allison did not fully consider Michael's and Joseph's concerns about their parents' desire that they stay close to home, noting that going away strengthened her relationships with her own parents; while that certainly might have been the case for Allison, we cannot assume the same will be true for Michael and Joseph. Educators must recognize that just because they experienced college a particular way does not mean their students will have those same experiences. For example, as Wilson (as cited in Kohli & Pizarro, 2016) noted, communities of Color often emphasize collective, rather than individual, achievement. As a result, students may be expected to continue to live with their parents after graduating from high school so that they may continue to contribute as active members of their family's day-to-day experience, a more difficult task for youth who leave home to live on campus. For educators to engage in culturally relevant college talk, they need to develop understandings of youth's cultural backgrounds and perspectives, and how they are similar to and different from educators' own experiences.

Another educator, Willard, a Black science teacher, discussed how he began drawing from his own experiences in his college talk with students during class time as a way to make connections to their experiences. In a focus group interview he shared:

> Well, sometimes I bring it from my own personal life. I tell them, I told them about the conversation I just had with one of my sisters-in-law and just discussing what are our plans for paying for my daughter's college tuition. And I discussed it with students, how are you going to help your parents support you and your aspirations to go to college because the rising costs of college puts a lot of people in debt. Therefore we started talking about internships or scholarships and how to think toward the future and really know that it's right around the corner. Sometimes even for myself, you get caught up in the day-to-day work ethic and it takes your eyes off the idea that it's moving forward to college and high school is just one step and you're supposed to be moving in that direction. (Interview)

Willard explicitly names how his own experiences as the parent of a soon-to-be college student influence the content of his college talk with students. Moreover, Willard notes the importance of taking time to engage in college talk with students throughout the school day, even as "you get caught up in the day-to-day work ethic." While educators may find it challenging to enact college talk in their daily interactions with students, Willard's noting that "you're supposed to be moving in that direction" reminds us of the importance of building on educators' daily interactions with students in ways that support their college readiness and access, particularly through instances of college talk. One additional point about Willard's comment above is that he shares a specific message in the college talk he described. In talking explicitly about options for paying for college, Willard is sharing specific information about internships and scholarships. This is information that some students may not have access to otherwise, as evidenced by our own conversations with high school youth who know that paying for college can create challenges but are less familiar with particular options that may exist to help make college more affordable. In beginning to consider how their lived experiences influenced their college talk with students, educators shared deepening understandings of the role they play in facilitating or hindering youth's access to information about preparing for, applying to, and/or enrolling in college.

Considerations of Fear Across Notions of Student Learning and Achievement

Even as the educators we collaborated with came to understand the role their own experiences and perspectives played in talking with youth about college, many experienced difficulties in recognizing that their college talk with Black and Latino young men may reflect their low expectations for students' academic achievement built on their misperceptions of students' fears. Elliot, a teacher at the High School for Investigation and Inquiry, provides one example. During a large-group discussion, Elliot noted:

> I think the juniors are terrified about college. A lot of them. A large swath of them. A lot of them skipped the PSAT. Um, and we make a big deal of it. We review with them, which I didn't do last year. I don't know how many of them took it last year either, but in my own proctoring room almost half of the class that was supposed to be there was not there. And it was just interesting 'cause I see it in their eyes. A lot of these boys that are really, over half of the junior class has a 65 average. They're really low and their skills are not so hot. So I'm trying to reconcile this with all these . . . 'cause it's been a little bit of a shocker for me to see that response and then realize this is a big deal [challenging] to a lot of them. Like things like putting their heads down [during test preparation and/or the exam]. [I'm] trying to get through and some of them are connecting.

Elliot's comments point to a number of concerns that educators across the CRE-PD shared. First, he notes that even though he and other educators in the school are "making a big deal" of the PSAT and other college-readiness activities, he is troubled by what he perceives as a lack of engagement on the part of students, particularly "these boys," as he refers to them. From Elliot's perspective, he is spending time preparing students for the PSAT, yet students are "putting their heads down," or choosing not to be present for the exam, which he interprets as a sign of disinterest on the part of the students. Building from notions of culturally relevant education leads us to view the situation Elliot described differently—from a perspective that builds on students' emotions and experiences with testing. Therefore, rather than say that students are "really low and their skills are not so hot," we ask what Elliot might do to allay some of students' perceived fears about high-stakes college admissions exams.

While educators may think they are demonstrating high expectations for youth's achievement by providing them with access to PSAT preparation materials, for example, their college talk sends a different message. Youth we have collaborated with tell us they know when they are being positioned negatively, particularly when their strengths and interests are not seen as a platform from which to build academic success in school. If more than half of the Back and Latino young men in Elliot's school really are earning a 65 average in their courses, we argue that educators should re-evaluate their curriculum and teaching practices to better meet the needs of students rather than continuing to expect students who are not experiencing success to adapt to current practices. For example, inequitable teaching practices or inaccessible curriculum may create conditions in which students fail. While educators' high expectations for student achievement are an important aspect of culturally relevant educational practices, when students' cultures and perspectives are not built upon in curriculum and teaching, the reason for failure may lie in the practices and structures rather than in the students themselves.

Autobiographical Reflection—Joanne

As a public high school teacher working in New York City, I often overheard my colleagues tell students that no one was going to "hold their hand" when they got to college. It was a statement often made in a moment of frustration or exasperation, when students had not completed a homework assignment, or forgot to bring the books or materials they needed for that day's class. Students who arrived late to school often received a similar message, hearing that no one would be there to wake them up in time for class as college students so they needed to learn now how to get themselves up and ready for school on time. Yet, rather than have the intended effect of encouraging students to engage in behaviors they would need for college while still in high school, many of the students I worked with said such college talk actually discouraged them from going to college, positioning college as a scary place they should be afraid of because—unlike their high school—no one in college would care whether they succeeded or failed. For example, if they experienced challenges in remembering to bring their homework assignments to school or in waking up on time while they were in high school and their teachers and families reminded them to do so, how could they do it on their own when they got to college and no one was there to assist them? This college talk is not only damaging to students' perceptions of their ability to succeed in college, it is also not entirely accurate. While it is true that Black and Latino young men continue to graduate from college at rates lower than those of other racial and ethnic groups, colleges and universities across the country have increasingly developed institutional structures seeking to support youth of Color as they make the transition from high school to college. Moreover, as college professors ourselves who have worked with undergraduate students we—and many of our colleagues—demonstrate an ethic of care toward our students, following up with them should they experience difficulty with class assignments, and referring students to campus writing centers and social organizations to support their transition to college. While students certainly need to demonstrate a certain level of independence as college students, college talk that describes college as a place where students will be left alone to succeed or fail without any chance of accessing support is not productive. Rather than scare students into doing well in high school by juxtaposing their current schooling experiences with what they may encounter in college, educators may instead make visible to students the social and institutional barriers and supports they may experience, and share strategies for negotiating them.

Sociopolitical Awareness

Once we better understood the expectations educators held for their students' academic achievement, we were able to guide them in considering how they might engage in more purposeful and culturally relevant college talk that shared high expectations for students' college-going futures. One strategy we used involved asking educators to consider whether the college talk they engaged in with students was reflective of structures that were consistent and equitable. For example, Marcy noted in a group discussion that she often engaged in college talk with Antonio, a student who came by her classroom after school had ended, but before the evening remedial courses he was taking began. She said:

> Like one student I'll see on Wednesdays, he had night class, a credit recovery. So he would see me in the hour before he would go to that credit recovery. So I knew that on Wednesdays I would see this particular student. I would tell him to write down, they each had a little book that they kept where they could write down questions . . . they could be home thinking about that question, write it down so that way when we meet we can go over it. Whether it's dealing with financial aid . . . and just making sure I kept a folder with any information I got, any emails. Make sure they signed up for like the FAFSA [Free Application for Federal Student Aid] day for the students that applied to SUNY. So make sure that their parents and them could attend, because that's a really informative meeting. And so, I think for me, it was about being consistent on a weekly basis in terms of making sure we follow through. (Focus group interview, 5/23/2014)

Even though Antonio was enrolled in a remedial course, Marcy positioned him as college-bound, demonstrating high expectations for his academic achievement. She also was specific in the conversations she had with

Antonio, using his notebook as a tool for him to write down questions throughout the week that they could discuss on Wednesday afternoons. In noting that the two talked about financial aid, FAFSA forms, and college applications, Marcy demonstrates purposeful college talk that highlights a specific example of the role individual teachers may play in reducing inequitable educational opportunities. However, we encouraged educators to collaborate with colleagues to consider the creation of school structures that could more equitably engage students in college talk. For example, while the college talk Marcy engaged in with Antonio was consistent, taking place every Wednesday after school, if Marcy had not chosen to stay after school, she and Antonio would not have had the opportunity to talk with each other. Additional students who could have benefitted from the kinds of college talk happening between Marcy and Antonio after school did not necessarily have access to those conversations, particularly if they were unable to stay after school. Adding opportunities for college talk to take place during the school day as part of a class or an advisory session could create access to college talk for more students.

Marcy was not the only educator we worked with who experienced success in making her college talk more specific, even as she continued to need support in making it more equitable. For example, Ricky described how his engagement in the professional development initiative led him to be more specific in his college talk with students. He said:

> Maybe it was just more in the forefront of my mind. 'Cause I typically
> . . . like, there was a kid that I had last year who I would always
> say I think he'd be a great attorney based on his argumentative and
> debating skills. And um, you know I'd call him esquire and we'd play
> around in the hallways with that, and then I don't know if I ever made
> the direct link for him, like, how do you get there? But because now
> it's in the forefront of my mind, I actually had a conversation with him
> just last week, and we talked about those steps and what direction
> he's going to go in. Because he's a kid who has the potential to go
> anywhere. It could be good and it could be really not. (Focus group
> interview, 5/23/2014)

In noting the importance of being more specific in his college talk, Ricky provides an example of steps educators can take to engage in more purposeful conversations with Black and Latino young men about college. Yet this example, similar to Marcy's conversations with Antonio, is centered in informal conversations that all students may not have access to, particularly those who have not developed relationships with adults in their school communities.

In addition to shifting college talk to be more specific, educators shared that they also considered the role their interactions with and expectations for students played in their conversations with them. After engaging in the professional development initiative, for example, Andrew shared in a focus group interview that the content of his college talk with students changed. He said:

> I really think it's rewording and rethinking what we say to kids. I think sometimes because the kids are not performing academically or socially where we want them to be, we kinda shut down and we kinda get the attitude that someone else will deal with it. I think now people realize that this area of the school is a part of the problem. And the things you say to a kid can make or break them. You might have an outburst with a kid one day, the next day is a new day. And I think that attitudinal shift in knowing these are kids, they have issues, I'm not going to let yesterday dictate today. A kid might have cursed me out and said everything about my wife and kids, but the next day, "Hey, Hi, How you doing?" Still building that relationship and letting them know that we're here for them and that we're not holding any grudges. I think a lot of these kids, a lot of things have not gone their way in life, they kinda feel that we're really not genuine in what we say. So I think people need to be more cognizant of that, even on their worst day. (Focus group interview, 5/23/2014)

In noting the role relationships (discussed in Chapter 4) play in enacting purposeful college talk supportive of Black and Latino young men's academic achievement, Andrew demonstrated how his perspective shifted as a result of his critical reflection. Rather than positioning students as singularly responsible for their engagement in school, Andrew noted that educators who choose not to "let yesterday dictate today" create opportunities for youth to meet high expectations for their achievement in school. Naming and repeating those high expectations provide a foundation from which intentional and culturally relevant college talk necessarily builds.

CONNECTING TO CLASSROOMS, SCHOOL CULTURE, AND COLLEGE ACCESS

Below, we share three strategies educators enacted to engage in more purposeful and equitable college talk with students across contexts of curriculum and teaching, school culture, and college readiness and access. Each strategy provides a practical way for educators to build on the tenets of culturally relevant pedagogy—student learning and achievement, cultural competence, and sociopolitical consciousness—in ways that assist them in enacting purposeful, equitable college talk with their Black and Latino male students.

Focus on Curriculum and Teaching

A promising action educators took to create more-equitable opportunities for engaging in purposeful college talk with students was to build such conversations into their courses. Maria provided an example, noting:

> Personally, in my classroom, we had chats. We would have Friday chats. The last 15 minutes, they would jot down questions they would have for me. Or maybe they had a personal experience they wanted to share with the class . . . on Fridays after we finished the lesson. I would leave a slot of time and I would do the Friday chats. But we've had some things come up where we can't do that because of time. And we're getting toward crunch time . . . toward Regents prep time. You know? So I feel like now, we're not able to really [enact] our action plans because now we have another focus. (Focus group interview, 5/23/2014)

Even as Maria noted the challenges she experienced in enacting purposeful college talk on a weekly basis with students, the practice provided a structure for equitable college talk to take place. In addition to the conversations Maria had with youth before or after class as an avenue for engaging in college talk, she also included such conversations with youth as an activity that took place during the courses she taught. This practice created space for students to ask and respond to questions on a more consistent basis. Although the Friday chats became less frequent with the onset of state exam preparation, Maria's action provides an example of possibilities for enacting more-equitable college talk with youth through the development of classroom structures.

Focus on School Culture

It is important for educators to collaborate with one another to develop shared understandings of the role college talk may play in supporting youth's academic achievement and engagement in school. Moreover, shared understandings of college talk are necessary for educators to convey consistent messages about college to youth (McClafferty et al., 2002). As a first step toward developing such shared understandings, we invited educators to collectively consider the college talk they engage in with students, and to consider whether youth's future careers are included in their conversations. In an interview after his participation in the CRE-PD ended, a Black male teacher noted:

> We don't have a collective you know, um, I should say, agreement of what our college readiness is in the school. Like everyone has different

ideas and that's something we need to strive to do, to try and have
a uniform kind of idea of what it is and what it looks like to further
help our students. I think that's the biggest thing that resonated with
me. (Interview)

One opportunity for supporting educators in sharing consistent messages through their college talk involves inventorying the visual representations of college-going practices in their school communities. Images, such
as displays indicating which colleges students have gained admission to, can
serve as entry points to enacting college talk. We therefore encouraged educators to consider whether and how the visual images of college readiness
and access in their schools were culturally relevant. One educator, Melissa,
used images depicting her own pathway to college as a way to make visible
the steps she took to pursue multiple college degrees. In a focus group interview, she shared:

> I remember thinking I would, since my office is a place a lot of
> students come to for support, that I would post more college-ready
> stuff up in the room. I've done one thing. Like I put up . . . a little
> poster that goes through my footsteps. So it goes through, you know
> I have two undergrads and two graduate degrees. So just the trail of
> the schools. So that's posted so kids will ask about that sometimes.
> . . . You know one may be enough. I just have to have more discussion
> about it with those students who come to me.—Melissa (5/23/14)

While Melissa chose to share only one visual element related to college
going in her office, doing so created an entry point for her to talk with students about her own pathway to college. We consider this action as providing an opportunity for students to consider how their own path to college
may be similar to or different from Melissa's path. Moreover, in outlining
the specific steps she took to earn several college degrees, Melissa shared
specific information with students rather than more general information
that might be less helpful to students' considerations of college-going.

Focus on College and Career Readiness

As indicated across the educator perspectives shared in this chapter, some
of the teachers and school leaders we collaborated with in the CRE-PD
experienced challenges in demonstrating high expectations for all of their
students in terms of ability and interest in attending college. Often, these
limited expectations for youth's futures were apparent in their college talk
or were enacted implicitly through positioning youth who were not meeting academic expectations as career ready without specifically identifying
what those careers might be or how students could pursue them. Yet, it is

necessary for culturally relevant educators to maintain high expectations for youth's academic achievement in ways that encourage students to navigate barriers to their college readiness and access, even as schooling structures may not create conditions that foster youth's success. For example, when educators consider particular youth not to be college-bound, they may offer them fewer opportunities to participate in daily activities—such as a rigorous academic curriculum, extracurricular activities, or access to information about preparing for and/or applying to college—that may support youth's engagement in school.

Robbie, a teacher at Collaboration Central High School, developed a schoolwide structure to more equitably provide access to information about professional careers that the Black and Latino young men he taught might pursue. As part of the action plan he developed and enacted during his participation in the CRE-PD, Robbie brought a group of male students on a class trip to NBC studios where they were able to interact with men of Color who worked there. In facilitating students' interaction with professionals who shared cultural and/or linguistic backgrounds with the youth, Robbie created opportunities for youth to learn about what it was like to be a Black or Latino male working in television, while at the same time demonstrating his high expectations for their futures. In addition, we argue that educators and students need more access to information about postsecondary pathways to careers that youth may wish to pursue. As an educator at Amsterdam High School noted, "We need a career fair. Not just people who went to Harvard. Plumber, video gaming, carpenter" (3/26/15). Providing information about certificates and credentials required for careers that do not require a 4-year college degree is an additional way educators may support students' access to postsecondary pathways.

CONCLUSION

Throughout this chapter, we have shared insights into the challenges and tensions that emerged when educators considered the individual and collective messages they sent to youth in their college talk. Specifically, we considered educators' reflections of their own college-going experiences as one way to demonstrate the importance of considering similarities and differences across race, ethnicity, culture, gender, and socioeconomic status when engaging in college talk with Black and Latino young men. Despite some educators placing responsibility for youth's academic achievement and engagement solely upon students without considering the role educators' expectations or inequitable school structures may play, we remain encouraged. As reflected in Andrew's comments earlier in this chapter, educators who participated in the CRE-PD grew to understand the important role educators can play in supporting youth's academic achievement, engagement in school, and college readiness through their enactment of consistent and strengths-based college talk with youth. We offer the recommendations and suggestions below to further support educators in taking action to create more-equitable learning opportunities for Black and Latinx youth across their college talk.

QUESTIONS AND ACTIONS FOR INDIVIDUALS AND SMALL GROUPS WITHIN SCHOOL COMMUNITIES

1. Reflect on the past several conversations you have had with Black and Latinx students about college. When, where, and how did those conversations take place? For example, who initiated each conversation? How often do conversations with the same students take place? After reflecting, talk with your colleagues and ask them to share their own reflections about instances of college talk. Together, consider when, where, and with whom college talk typically happens. What messages are shared? How might college talk be regularly and equitably incorporated into your individual and collective interactions with students? How do these conversations reflect the three tenets of culturally relevant pedagogy?
2. Talk with youth about when, where, and how they typically engage in college talk with one another. How can you build from youth's culturally relevant peer interactions (see Chapter 5) to support students' achievement in high school and preparation for college?
3. Make a list of the information you need in order to more purposefully engage in college talk with students. For example, are you confident in your understandings about the various types of postsecondary institutions that may best serve your students? What aspects of college application or financial aid processes could you benefit from learning more about?
4. Visually, what in your school's institutional culture serves as a catalyst for college talk? How might educators collaborate to visually forefront collective college-going identities that create entry points for all students in a school community to talk with one another and with educators about preparing for and applying to college?

CHAPTER 7

Conclusion

Throughout this book, we have argued that culturally relevant educational practices provide a necessary framework for supporting educators in ensuring that they are facilitating access to opportunities for the students of Color with whom they work. Efforts to more equitably teach youth of Color are particularly urgent because schools in urban, rural, and suburban communities are experiencing increases in the population of culturally and linguistically diverse children, youth, and families they serve. As the nation's demographics continue to shift, it is necessary for educators to develop nuanced understandings of the perspectives of youth of Color in ways that reflect the heterogeneity of their experiences, and intersections of multiple identities such as gender, social class, language, and immigrant status.

We argued that educators must examine, reflect upon, and seek to understand their own identities so they are better positioned to understand and teach all students, particularly students of Color. Such work requires educators to engage in uncovering and challenging stereotypes while recognizing and building upon students' strengths. Further, enacting strengths-based perspectives supports educators in developing culturally relevant practices that lead to productive relationships between teachers and students, and between students and their peers. Moreover, educators' purposeful college talk supports the college-going identities, college readiness, and future career possibilities of youth of Color. Undergirding these arguments are the ways in which these culturally relevant practices support students' learning and achievement, create a school culture that is responsive to the needs of students, and promote the college and career readiness of Black and Latinx youth.

Now, in this concluding chapter, we call for educators to engage in ongoing critical reflection about their curriculum, teaching, school policies, and school structures by examining their work in relation to the tenets of culturally relevant pedagogy. We also provide recommendations for school leaders seeking to enact necessary change in educational opportunities, college enrollment, and future career opportunities for youth of Color.

RECOMMENDATIONS FOR EDUCATORS

The recommendations that follow are meant to serve as a starting point—not an exhaustive list—for educators seeking to disrupt inequitable opportunities that exist in their classroom and school communities. These are practices that can be taken up in schools serving any number of youth of Color across multiple school contexts. Many of the recommendations we provide are meant to be enacted by large groups of educators, including colleagues across entire school communities. However, we have met teachers in multiple contexts who share that they are still working to identify colleagues willing to collaborate in challenging inequitable educational opportunities encountered by students in their schools. Therefore we intentionally have provided recommendations that may be taken up by individual educators as well.

Our recommendations are grouped according to one of the three tenets of culturally relevant pedagogy that most directly applies to the action we call upon educators to enact. That said, we recognize that much of the work we describe below involves aspects of more than one culturally relevant tenet at a time. We encourage educators to refer to the list of culturally relevant indicators provided in Appendix B as a way to gain a more nuanced understanding of whether and how particular practices they seek to enact in their classrooms and school communities include elements of the three tenets of culturally relevant pedagogy: student learning and achievement, cultural competence, and sociopolitical awareness. We begin each of the sections that follow by sharing insights gained from our work with educators, before providing specific recommendations that may be taken up across multiple contexts.

Student Learning and Achievement

For educators to realize schoolwide academic achievement and college readiness, they must enact equitable schooling practices that support the learning and achievement of culturally and linguistically diverse youth. Such work is a multifaceted endeavor situated across multiple contexts within school communities. For example, some educators we worked with in the CRE-PD sought to ensure that exemplar student work posted on bulletin boards throughout the school included an equitable representation of assignments completed by youth of Color, particularly Black and Latino male students who were under-represented in an initial inventory of displayed student work. Other educators organized special assemblies or fieldtrips to workplaces featuring guest speakers who shared their experiences working in fields and positions that students of Color might aspire to. Yet even as educators sought to increase educational opportunity for their students of Color, we were struck by how often those opportunities—including those described above—were situated beyond the walls of their content-area classrooms.

We see multiple paths forward for supporting educators in enacting curriculum and teaching that more explicitly take into consideration the learning and achievement of culturally and linguistically diverse youth. We recommend, as a step in that direction, that educators consider the experiences of particular students who experience inequitable opportunities in their school communities and then take up the actions and questions below individually, in conversation with colleagues who teach the same content area or grade level, or as a whole-school community.

1. *Examine instances of achievement.* Consider the circumstances of the culturally and linguistically diverse students who most often engaged and/or experienced achievement in your classroom, or the classrooms of your colleagues. What adjustments could you make to your curriculum and teaching to replicate those circumstances? While considering the heterogeneity of students' experiences, examine how particular groups of students, such as Black male students, Latinx students, or English language learners, experience curriculum and teaching. Find time to talk with students you are seeking to better support about whether they agree with your findings, and to invite their ideas for how you might better support their learning and engagement.

2. *Reconsider how you ask students to demonstrate their understanding of course concepts and/or content.* For example, does learning tend to take place when students work independently on assignments at home, or collaboratively with peers during class? Provide a variety of opportunities for students to demonstrate what they learn in ways that simultaneously meet course goals and build from students' strengths.

3. *Support collective notions of achievement.* Provide whole-class incentives such as a class celebration or visit to a college or workplace to encourage students to support one another's academic achievement in the context of your course. For example, create classroom resources that students can share with absent classmates over social media, or reward those who share information about community events or college preparatory activities that may be of interest to additional students in the class.

4. *Create opportunities in the curriculum for students to examine their educational experiences.* Youth Participatory Action Research (YPAR) provides meaningful opportunities for students to apply course content to their lived experiences (Caraballo et al., 2017; Fine, Torre, Burns, & Payne, 2007; Warren & Marciano, 2018). Consider how your course might address content-area learning

standards by asking students to pose and examine research questions related to the content area you teach. For example, a YPAR project that supports students in examining how school-funding policies impact physical, monetary, and intellectual resources available in various schools across their communities holds potential for extending, in meaningful ways, content knowledge in math, history, geography, science, and English.

5. *Talk with students about their interests and goals.* Engaging in conversations with youth about their interests and goals outside of school can create opportunities for building connections to course content. Consider how you might incorporate ideas and activities students find engaging into your daily teaching practices. In addition, consider ways you might incorporate into the curriculum current events that could connect to youth's experiences, such as the Black Lives Matter and #MeToo movements.

6. *Make explicit connections between classroom experiences and college readiness.* Including college talk in curriculum and pedagogy creates structures for students to ask questions, collaborate, and develop future-oriented college identities. For example, invite students in a math course to examine multiple ways of calculating the costs associated with attending college, or support students' discussion skills by asking them to interview community members about their own college-going experiences.

Cultural Competence

In considering issues of cultural competence, we found it important to facilitate conversations that supported educators in considering how their own experiences as students influenced their teaching and students' learning. Educators of varying racial, ethnic, and socioeconomic statuses held assumptions about culturally and linguistically diverse youth that influenced their work. These assumptions often were grounded in educators' own experiences as students, or in their interactions with groups of Black, Latinx, immigrant, and/or linguistically diverse students. For example, teachers discussed how they grew up in circumstances similar to those of their students, questioned students' lack of engagement in juxtaposition to their own academic achievement, or positioned groups of students as uninterested in achieving academically or engaging in school, even as individual students experienced success. In examining their own multiple and intersecting identities, educators were better able to understand that students brought their own varied experiences and perspectives into their interactions. Such understandings supported educators in creating more-equitable schooling experiences for students that drew on their cultural experiences as strengths.

In implementing action plans in their school communities, educators experienced varying levels of success in learning about and building from youth's cultural experiences. For example, many educators developed advisory sessions that required youth of Color, specifically Black and Latino young men, to interact with one another and discuss future goals, such as college access. While creating spaces for youth to be in conversation with one another can provide opportunities for the sharing of their cultural experiences, we argue that it is necessary to more explicitly position educators as learners in those spaces. The recommendations below provide starting points for educators working individually and collaboratively to take action to learn about their students' cultural experiences in ways that may create more-equitable schooling experiences for youth of Color.

1. *Name your assumptions.* Although it can be difficult to explicitly name assumptions you may hold about culturally and linguistically diverse youth, doing so is an important first step in examining whether, how, and why those assumptions influence your work with students. Do these assumptions reflect asset-based or deficit-based perspectives of diverse racial/ethnic student populations? After naming your assumptions, consider their sources. For example, in what ways do your previous interactions with Black and Latino young men, and representations of them in news media and popular culture, influence your ideas about their experiences and interests? Focusing on multiple media representations of multiple demographic groups of students in your school community may provide more nuanced understandings of the similarities and differences experienced by youth of Color with whom you work.

2. *Examine your assumptions.* Talk with your colleagues and students to challenge your assumptions. For example, in Chapter 6 we described an educator who stated that most of the Black and Latino male students in his school earned an overall average of 65%. Do the data support that assumption? When, how, and why? Look at the grades youth of Color earn in the courses you teach and/or in all of the courses they are enrolled in. What trends do you notice in the data? How are individual students' experiences reflected (or not) in those trends? What might educators need to do differently if most of the Black and Latino male students in a school are, in fact, earning grades of 65%?

3. *Talk with youth.* We found one of the most effective ways for educators to develop cultural competence was to engage in conversations with youth about what their lived experiences were. These conversations may take place across informal and formal contexts, such as before and after class, in assignments

that ask students to reflect on their experiences and perspectives, and during fieldtrips, lunchtime conversations, or extracurricular activities.

4. **Build from youth's strengths.** After naming and examining your assumptions, and talking with students about their experiences, use what you learned to build from youth's strengths and create more-equitable educational opportunities. For example, if youth explain that they enjoy working with peers during class activities, facilitate opportunities for those engagements to take place in courses you teach. Make connections between youth's in-school and out-of-school experiences, building from what youth tell you they are interested in, rather than what you assume they are interested in.

5. **Create opportunities for youth to learn from the college-going experiences of their peers.** Invite school alumni of differing racial/ethnic, classed, and linguistic backgrounds to return to your school community to talk about both the successes and challenges of attending college. Facilitate honest discussions about students' fears associated with attending college, including how cultural and linguistic diversity (or lack of diversity) on college campuses may influence youth's experiences.

6. **Recognize that developing cultural competence is an ongoing endeavor.** To develop as culturally competent educators, we must engage in continual, critical reflection of our assumptions about youth's multiple and varied cultural experiences. How might you engage in continued reflection and/or discussion with colleagues about whether, how, and why your interactions with youth build from their strengths in ways that support more-equitable educational opportunities?

Sociopolitical Consciousness

Culturally relevant educators "seek to empower students so that they may disrupt existing power structures" (Royal & Gibson, 2017, p. 11). However, for educators to develop and extend the sociopolitical consciousness of their students, they must be able to understand and work to disrupt those existing structures themselves. One of the most prevalent assumptions we encountered in our work with educators throughout the CRE-PD was that individual students were solely responsible for their success and/or failure in school. We found that many educators' own schooling experiences influenced their assumptions about whether, how, and why youth of Color, particularly Black and Latino young men, engaged with school. Teachers talked about their own academic performance or participation in extracurricular activities as the standard to which students should aspire. Often, these comparisons did not consider the institutional structures that supported educators in experiencing success. Moreover, educators who achieved academically across their own schooling experiences tended to encounter tensions as they considered the role they played in facilitating or hindering the schooling experiences of youth of Color. Specifically, students who did not actively participate in class often were positioned as disengaged, removing the responsibility for supporting their learning from educators. However, initially left unconsidered were institutional structures, limited access to resources, and deficit-oriented stereotypes about culturally and linguistically diverse youth that influenced their access to equitable learning opportunities.

To support educators in developing an awareness of the institutional and social structures that prevent youth of Color from having access to equitable educational experiences, we call upon educators to engage in ongoing critical reflection of their lived experiences and those of their students. For example, in asking educators to reflect on their own cultural backgrounds as well as the assumptions they may hold about students of Color, we discovered entry points for supporting educators in reconsidering these assumptions. We offer the suggestions and recommendations below as specific, actionable steps educators can take to develop and/or further extend their own sociopolitical consciousness, and to extend that consciousness to their work with culturally and linguistically diverse youth.

1. *Identify and reflect on the societal and/or institutional structures that have made your own achievements possible.* Consider some of the achievements you have accomplished throughout your life, such as graduating from high school and college or experiencing success as an educator. Who and what supported you in achieving those accomplishments? What challenges did you encounter? How might you make those structures visible to youth when talking with them about your own educational and work experiences?

2. *Name and address barriers to students' academic achievement.* Inequitable schooling opportunities often result from social and institutional structures that limit youth's access to information and experiences that may support their academic achievement. Teach students to consider such barriers, and to take action to address them. For example, punitive school policies (e.g., zero-tolerance versus restorative practices) that prevent students from participating in learning activities because they arrived late to school hinder students' academic engagement. How might new policies be imagined and enacted that better support youth in gaining access to equitable schooling experiences?

3. *Understand that supporting youth's sociopolitical consciousness is an ongoing process that includes your own critical self-reflection.* Each group of students we work with reminds us of the multiple and varied experiences encountered by youth. As the sociopolitical landscape across the United States continues to change, educators must remain in conversation with youth about their lived experiences and perspectives. Work to develop relationships with youth that allow you to recognize and build on their strengths, and to consider barriers to their academic success and achievement.

4. *Connect to college and career opportunities.* Engage in college talk with youth that demystifies the challenges they may encounter when applying for, enrolling in, and attending college and/or pursuing future careers. For example, educators may introduce students to support services available on college campuses, such as writing centers, mentoring programs, and advising services, that exist to directly address inequitable educational opportunities that otherwise could create barriers to students' academic achievement. Providing information to students about postsecondary pathways to careers is another promising practice, particularly for students who may want to explore options for future careers.

5. *Be aware.* In changing political times, educators must be aware of how government policies, particularly those related to language and citizenship status, affect students' access to educational opportunity, including college and future careers. For example, educators who work with undocumented immigrant students and their families should be knowledgeable about college and career opportunities that may be influenced by students' citizenship status.

6. *Take action.* Educators we worked with across the CRE-PD shared that developing and enacting action plans assisted them in creating more-equitable learning opportunities for Black and Latino male students. Consider specific changes you can make to your curriculum, pedagogy, and/or school structures that could build on youth's strengths and challenge inequities they encounter, while supporting their engagement in school.

RECOMMENDATIONS FOR SCHOOL LEADERS

The following recommendations provide starting points for school administrators, including those working at district, regional, and state levels, to create professional development opportunities across multiple contexts toward enacting necessary change in educational opportunities, college enrollment, and future career opportunities for youth of Color.

Create Professional Development Opportunities Centered on CRE

Creating more-equitable educational opportunities for culturally and linguistically diverse youth requires ongoing professional development focused on deepening and extending educators' understanding and enactment of culturally relevant educational practices. We recommend that school leaders and policymakers consider the professional development opportunities they currently offer educators to examine how inequities related to race, ethnicity, social class, gender, language, and additional identities are being addressed. For example, we are encouraged by New York City's recent decision to respond to "instances of racism in public schools" by investing $23 million to provide professional development for public school educators focused on anti-bias training and culturally responsive educational practices (Chapman, 2018). Such efforts necessarily bring considerations of race, ethnicity, and culture to the center of attempts to reduce educational inequities across school communities in ways that are attentive to the heterogeneity of youth's lived experiences.

Enact a Schoolwide Inquiry-Oriented Approach

We encourage school leaders to create institutional structures that provide time and space for educators to collaborate as they engage in professional development focused on CRE. As we noted in Chapter 1, even educators who began the CRE-PD familiar with notions of culturally relevant education, experienced challenges in defining what it looked like in their classrooms and school communities. Moreover, educators shared varying definitions of the term *culture*. Through their consistent engagement in the CRE-PD, educators were able to spend time grappling with these considerations while learning from and with colleagues. The involvement of their school administrators in the PD sessions also was cited by educators as supporting their own engagement. We therefore argue for school leaders to participate in CRE-PD alongside educators in their schools, or with leaders from other school buildings, as a way to demonstrate their willingness and commitment to this work. Moreover, educators shared that participating in the multiple professional development sessions we facilitated held them accountable for taking action between our scheduled sessions. For example, educators shared that they enacted action plans they created during CRE-PD sessions because they knew that during our next session together they would have to share reflections of what they learned. Such shared expectations for engagement in professional development, modeled by both educators and school leaders, further supported educators' participation in the CRE-PD.

Consider Varied Contexts for Enacting CRE

While we facilitated the CRE-PD in public secondary schools in New York City, findings shared throughout this book may influence the practices of educators who work with culturally and linguistically diverse youth in a variety of school contexts. We encourage educational leaders to be in conversation with the educators they work with to identify students who are experiencing educational inequities. Once students have been identified, educators may consider multiple ways to enact culturally relevant educational practices to support them. For example, some educators may seek to better understand the schooling experiences of the refugee students they serve, while others could work to better support linguistically diverse students. Moreover, educators who teach in school contexts with smaller numbers of culturally and linguistically diverse youth also should be encouraged to take up the practices described in this book and through their own participation in professional development focused on culturally relevant education. Creating entry points for educators to consider notions of culturally relevant educational practices for multiple groups of students across varied school contexts is an important step in challenging educational inequities.

Encourage Discomfort

Engaging in critical reflection about assumptions, stereotypes, and deficit-oriented perspectives about youth is not an easy task. As we noted in Chapter 3, educators experienced tension when we first asked them to name stereotypes based on race, ethnicity, and culture. Yet naming the assets and deficits typically ascribed to youth of Color, particularly Black and Latino young men, created entry points for educators to consider their own assumptions, and the role they played in creating inequitable schooling experiences for youth. By encouraging discomfort, school leaders can support educators as they grapple with the difficult task of reflecting on and challenging whether, how, and why they may be contributing to educational inequities.

Take Action

We purposefully chose to incorporate opportunities for educators to develop and enact action plans as an integral part of the CRE-PD. This inquiry approach created opportunities for educators to connect what they were learning in the CRE-PD to the classroom and school contexts in which they worked every day. We found that educators were most enthusiastic about their learning when we created opportunities to reflect upon their lived experiences and perspectives. In addition to fostering participants' engagement, educators' action plans provided opportunities for them to further develop their sociopolitical consciousness. By identifying inequities in their own school communities and taking action to address them, educators became more aware of the institutional structures that could facilitate or hinder the academic achievement and college readiness of the youth of Color with whom they worked.

LOOKING AHEAD

Culturally relevant educational practices provide an important foundation for the urgent and necessary work of increasing educational opportunities for culturally and linguistically diverse youth. However, the educators whose perspectives are featured throughout this book show us that understanding and enacting culturally relevant pedagogical practices is often a challenging endeavor. For teachers, guidance counselors, administrators, and staff working in schools where conversations about race, ethnicity, socioeconomic status, and educational inequities are not actively taken up, this work is perhaps even more challenging, and needed. It is our hope that the insights and perspectives shared throughout this book can serve as a starting point for individual and collective considerations of the work that must be done to address educational inequities in all contexts—rural, suburban, and urban—in which youth of Color engage in schooling.

Number and Roles of CRE-PD Participants

From 2013 to 2015, we collaborated with more than 500 teachers, guidance counselors, school administrators, and school support staff from 28 schools who participated in CRE-PD sessions we designed and facilitated. The tables that follow provide details about these educators and their school communities, organized by the date and location of their participation, and whether their participation was voluntary or required by their school administrators. For example, the tables indicate whether the CRE-PD sessions were held on campus at Teachers College, Columbia University, on-site at participating school sites, or at central locations chosen by the New York City Department of Education. Some of the school communities are included in more than one table to indicate participation in more than one date and/or location.

Table A1. Number and Roles of CRE-PD Participants, January/February 2013—At University

School	Number of PD Sessions	Percent Black and Latinx Students	Teachers	Counselors	Administrators	Support Staff	Total Participants
Academy of Peace and Justice*	6	94.9	0	0	0	2	2
Chester Academy	6	93.8	1	0	0	0	1
Collaboration C.H.S.*	6	97.3	3	1	0	1	5
Constitution H.S.*	6	98.4	1	0	1	0	2
Golden Ridge C.H.S.*	6	96.9	1	0	0	0	1
High School for Investigation and Inquiry*+	6	97.4	3	1	2	0	6
High School of Reform and Innovation*	6	100	1	0	0	0	1
Sussex Road School	6	83.8	0	1	0	0	1
Transformation Academy*	6	96.7	2	0	0	0	2
Total Number of Participants Across Schools	—	—	12	3	3	3	21

Note: Participant counts were taken for highest day of attendance across PD sessions. Percent Black and Latinx are for the 2012–2013 school year.
* Some schools appeared in multiple series to accommodate additional teachers within their schools.
+ Some school administrators required educators in their school building to attend the CRE-PD sessions.

Table A2. Number and Roles of CRE-PD Participants, August 2013—At University

School	Number of PD Sessions	Percent Black and Latinx Students	Teachers	Counselors	Administrators	Support Staff	Total Participants
Academy for Leadership	5	96.2	0	0	1	0	1
Academy of Peace and Justice*	5	94.9	1	0	0	1	2
Borough Academy*	5	98.3	1	0	0	0	1
Briarwood Prep	5	96	0	0	1	0	1
Career Success	5	80.8	0	0	0	1	1
Collaboration C.H.S.*	5	97.3	3	1	0	0	4
Constitution H.S.*	5	98.4	2	0	1	0	3
Eastern Prep Academy*	5	79.3	0	0	0	1	1
Golden Ridge C.H.S.*	5	96.9	1	0	0	0	1
High School for Career Advancement	5	90.2	0	0	1	0	1
High School for Investigation and Inquiry*	5	97.4	3	0	0	0	3
High School of Reform and Innovation*	5	100	1	0	0	0	1
Metropolitan High School*	5	92.6	1	0	0	0	1
Transformation Academy*	5	96.7	1	0	0	0	1
Washington High School	5	79.2	2	0	0	0	2
Total Number of Participants Across Schools	–	–	16	1	4	3	24

Note: Participant counts were taken for highest day of attendance across PD sessions. Percent Black and Latinx are for the 2012–2013 school year.
* Some schools appeared in multiple series to accommodate additional teachers within their schools.

Table A3. Number and Roles of CRE-PD Participants, September 2013–June 2014—On Site

School	Number of PD Sessions	Percent Black and Latinx Students	Teachers	Counselors	Administrators	Support Staff	Total Participants
Borough Academy*+	1	96.3	24	0	1	0	25
Buena Vista High School*+	4	81.0	13	2	2	2	19
City Leadership Academy	4	91.4	31	1	1	7	40
Civic High School	4	83.1	11	1	1	0	13
Constitution H.S.*	4	98.3	10	0	2	6	18
Eastern Prep Academy*+	2	82.0	82	0	0	4	86
Emily Dickenson Academy	1	95.6	40	3	3	7	53
Future Tech+	4	90.2	33	1	2	0	36
Harken High School	4	98.8	8	3	1	2	14
High School for Investigation and Inquiry*	4	96.9	23	1	3	0	27
Metropolitan High School*	4	91.5	13	0	1	2	16
Total Number of Participants Across Schools	–	–	288	12	17	30	347

Note: Participant counts were taken for highest day of attendance across PD sessions. Percent Black and Latinx are for the 2013–2014 school year.

* Some schools appeared in multiple series to accommodate additional teachers within their schools.

+ Some school administrators required educators in their school building to attend the CRE-PD sessions.

Table A4. Number and Roles of CRE-PD Participants, September 2014–June 2015—On Site

School	Number of PD Sessions	Percent Black and Latinx Students	Teachers	Counselors	Administrators	Support Staff	Total Participants
Amsterdam High	5	95.3	18	0	1	2	21
Borough Academy*+	1	95.3	17	0	1	5	23
Buena Vista High School*+	4	80.1	23	0	0	0	23
Coleman High School	4	95.8	25	0	2	0	27
Constitution H.S.*	4	97.4	23	0	2	10	35
Davis Academy of Technology	4	92.9	10	0	0	0	10
Eastern Prep Academy*	4	80.3	25	0	0	0	25
Eastern Prep Academy *+	1	80.3	75	0	1	0	76
Forte School	2	98.5	5	0	0	0	5
Metropolitan High School*	4	91.8	10	0	0	0	10
Thorndike High School+	4	98.7	23	0	2	0	25
Total Number of Participants Across Schools	–	–	254	0	9	17	280

Note: Participant counts were taken for highest day of attendance across PD sessions. Percent Black and Latinx are for the 2014–15 school year.
* Some schools appeared in multiple series to accommodate additional teachers within their schools.
+ Some school administrators required educators in their school building to attend the CRE-PD sessions.

CRE Indicators and College Readiness

How do your curricular and pedagogical practices and policies address the following indicators for CRE and college readiness? You can refer to the key below as you reflect on and respond to each practice that you use with your students.

Key: 1 = Always, 2 = Usually, 3 = Sometimes, 4 = Rarely, 5 = Never

Student Learning and Achievement—Academic, personal, and social experiences

___ 1.a. Sends consistent messages and clear expectations that all students can be prepared to be college ready and attend college.

___ 1.b. Discusses and supports students to take academically rigorous courses and tests that support students' options to attend a 4-year college as well as a range of postsecondary institutions (e.g., grades, PSAT/SAT/ACT).

___ 1.c. Targets and provides additional academic support based on individual progress (e.g., tutoring, organizational skills, study skills, creating individual academic plans).

___ 1.d. Engages students in active learning.

___ 1.e. Utilizes multiple assessments for academic, personal, and/or social success.

Cultural Competence—Cultural identities and background experiences for student learning and achievement

___ 2.a. Builds on students' prior knowledge and interest in the learning process across the school (e.g., the curriculum, extracurricular activities, student leadership, testing).

___ 2.b. Learns about students' culture and community and includes their cultural and academic identities as part of the learning process across the school (e.g., the curriculum, counseling office, parent/ family involvement).

___ 2.c. Understands and addresses the personal and cultural biases toward Black and Latinx youth and how they are viewed as college-bound or not (e.g., visual representations).

___ 2.d. Fosters meaningful relationships between student and school personnel by focusing and building on student's assets versus deficits.

___ 2.e. Fosters meaningful relationships between students and their peers as they influence student's academic success and college-going identities.

Critical Consciousness/Awareness—Knowledge of the college-going processes for student learning and achievement

___ 3.a. Demystifies the college-going process (e.g., course curriculum sequence, financial aid, campus visit) by disseminating information about college requirements, the application process, and important deadlines.

___ 3.b. Negotiates inconsistent messages between and among staff, and/ or students regarding clear expectations for college readiness.

___ 3.c. Addresses nonacademic concerns (e.g., personalized support for behaviors, peer pressure, violence).

___ 3.d. Discusses issues about race/ethnicity, gender, and achievement (e.g., Amir, Love Letter to Albuquerque Public Schools, questioning how many Black and Latino males enter a specific college and graduate).

___ 3.e. Provides opportunities for student voice and advocacy for their own learning (e.g., student leadership).

Methodology

Research Context

In 2012, Michelle Knight-Manuel and Joanne Marciano were invited by members of the New York City Department of Education's (NYC DOE) Office of Postsecondary Readiness to present findings from the study described in their book, *College Ready: Preparing Black and Latina/o Youth for Higher Education—A Culturally Relevant Approach* (Knight & Marciano, 2013). Four vendors, including Michelle and Joanne, were then invited to provide professional development beginning in January 2013 as part of the Expanded Success Initiative (ESI). The NYC DOE funded opportunities for educators at 40 high schools participating in the ESI to participate in any of the professional development provided by the four vendors with the purpose of providing daily meaningful educational experiences and increasing the college and career readiness of Black and Latino male students. To participate in the ESI, schools had to meet the following criteria: (1) at least 35% of enrollment was Black and Latino males; (2) at least 60% of enrolled students qualified for free and/or reduced lunch; and (3) the school graduated at least 65% of its students in 4 years. Although schools had 4-year graduation rates higher than the city's average, the schools eligible for inclusion had a substantially lower score, less than 12.5%, on a college readiness index (CRI). The CRI includes the percentage of students demonstrating a level of proficiency in reading, writing, and mathematics that allows them to avoid remedial coursework at local colleges. From January 2013 to Summer 2015, educators from 28 of the 40 high schools chose to participate in more in-depth culturally relevant professional development sessions (the CRE-PD) provided by Michelle and Joanne.

Professional Development Sessions

The PD sessions were developed and facilitated by Michelle and Joanne. We drew upon findings from an analysis of a 4-year ethnographic study of who and what influenced college-going practices of Black and Latinx working-class youth attending a NYC public high school and shared in our book

College Ready: Preparing Black and Latina/o Youth for Higher Education—A Culturally Relevant Approach (Knight & Marciano, 2013). Sessions were conducted after school, during the summer, and during in-service professional development days. Participants received payment from their schools to participate. CRE-PD sessions were designed to draw upon participants' experiences working with Black and Latino male students, and to highlight opportunities to connect research and practices that emphasized a strengths-based perspective. Specifically, sessions covered topics such as the definitions of culturally relevant education, students' assets versus deficits, examining racial/ethnic stereotypes, as well as applying indicators of culturally relevant college-going approaches to practice. Throughout the PD sessions, participants created and implemented weekly assignments and action plans, transforming PD material into classroom and schoolwide activities.

In addition to the CRE-PD sessions, we also met with ESI liaisons, school leaders, and teachers, from each of the 40 schools participating in the broader ESI program, and who met monthly as a group. During those district meetings, liaisons engaged in professional development aimed at supporting their schools' work with ESI. We facilitated 1-hour workshops on topics related to culturally relevant education and college and career readiness for an hour during each day-long session across 3 years. While this book focuses primarily on the professional development sessions in and across the 28 schools we collaborated with, we also draw from our work with the liaisons during those monthly sessions. ESI liaisons were teachers and administrators selected by their schools to facilitate communication between ESI and their school communities and support implementation of the ESI Initiative.

Positionality

It is important to understand our positionalities in relation to the professional development sessions we conducted and the study. Michelle Knight-Manuel is an African American educator who has been involved in teaching, working, and conducting culturally relevant research with teachers, students, families, communities, and teacher educators to create more-equitable and humane learning environments for minoritized students in Pennsylvania, California, and New York for over 30 years. Currently, she is involved with creating, facilitating, and researching after-school clubs for and with youth who are African immigrants and first-generation students. She is interested in understanding how they make sense of their notions of (civic) belonging and how these understandings can speak to the civic assets students bring to school and how they can speak to the "new" civics needed in our schools today.

Joanne Marciano is a White educator and researcher who has collaborated with youth, their families, preservice teachers, and inservice teachers across multiple educational contexts for the past 17 years in New York City and Michigan. Joanne's research engages qualitative participatory methodologies to highlight opportunities for supporting youth's literacy learning across contexts of secondary English education, urban education, and teacher education. Joanne's work continues to be informed by her experiences teaching secondary English for 13 years in a public high school in New York City. A central part of her research agenda involves highlighting opportunities for culturally and linguistically diverse youth to utilize Youth Participatory Action Research in examining how their schooling experiences are influenced by challenges and tensions that emerge when students encounter educational inequities.

Research Design

The purpose of this qualitative study was to examine how teachers, counselors, administrators, and school staff in 28 NYC public high schools who participated in the CRE-PD made sense of and enacted culturally responsive pedagogy in their classrooms and across the school culture, given the opportunity gaps among youth of Color, especially Black and Latino young men. Drawing on a range of data from culturally responsive education professional development implemented for 2 ½ to 3 years across 28 schools in New York City, we address the following questions: How do school staff experience culturally relevant education around high school completion and college readiness? What is the influence of culturally relevant education professional development workshops on their beliefs, knowledge, and practices?

Participants

A purposeful sample of more than 500 teachers, counselors, administrators, and support staff from 28 ESI schools participated in the CRE-PD (Bogdan & Biklen, 2007) from January 2013 to June 2015. In six of the 28 schools—Buena Vista High School, Coleman High School, Eastern Prep, Future Tech, High School for Investigation and Inquiry, and Thorndike High School—the principal required that either the entire staff or a group of teachers attend the CRE-PD. Because this book focuses on race, equity, and pedagogies, we note the importance of naming the ethnic identities of participants whenever possible. In many examples throughout this text, we have done so. However, in some instances, information about participants' racial/ethnic backgrounds was not available. For example, observation notes taken during PD sessions serving large numbers of educators did not always reference participants' racial and/or ethnic backgrounds. In addition, focus group interviews conducted by researchers working with the New York City Department of Education and shared with us as data sources did not include this information. Throughout this book, we have shared as much identifying information as possible each time we have referred to participants.

Data Collection and Analysis

The culturally diverse university research team consisted of one professor who is African American and six doctoral students: one Black female, one Black male, one Asian female, and three White females. The research team engaged in data collection and/or analysis as an ongoing, simultaneous, iterative process. Data collection was conducted by members of the Department of Education and the graduate students, who were familiar with CRE. Primary data collected consisted of a participant introductory questionnaire, observations of PD sessions, written documentation from activities facilitated throughout session activities such as school-based action plans, verbatim transcriptions of thirteen 30- to 45-minute focus group interviews that were conducted after each CRE-PD was completed, and evaluative feedback on each session. Other data sources included written documentation, archival data, and secondary data (e.g., DOE school report/ ESI websites, media reports, demographics). Research team members held collaborative discussions and wrote reflective memos after professional development sessions.

We drew upon our conceptual framework to code qualitative data for categories, patterns, and themes emerging across issues such as high expectations and support, teacher–student relationships, college-going conversations, assets versus deficits, and extracurricular activities. We looked for alternative examples within and across the data to highlight tensions within each theme (Bogdan & Biklen, 2007). We wrote memos on and across individual transcripts, and shared drafts among the multiple researchers. This process of analysis, rooted in data and researchers' reflexive work, strengthened the credibility, usefulness, and originality of findings.

References

Achinstein, B., & Aguirre, J. (2008). Cultural match or culturally suspect: How new teachers of color negotiate sociocultural challenges in the classroom. *Teachers College Record, 110*(8), 1505–1540.

Adichie, C. N. (2009). *The danger of a single story.* Retrieved from www.youtube .com/watch?v=D9Ihs241zeg

Allen, Q. (2015). Race, culture, and agency: Examining the ideologies and practices of U.S. teachers of Black male students. *Teaching and Teacher Education, 47*, 71–81.

Allen, K. M., Jackson, I., & Knight, M. G. (2012). Complicating culturally relevant pedagogy: Unpacking West African immigrants' cultural identities. *International Journal of Multicultural Education, 14*(2), 1–28.

Andrews, W. (2007). *Lots of "posse"-bilities.* United States: CBS News. Retrieved from www.youtube.com/watch?v=RV82M3wiJLc

Annamma, S., Jackson, D., & Morrison, D. (2017). Conceptualizing color-evasiveness: Using dis/ability critical race theory to expand a color-blind racial ideology in education and society. *Race Ethnicity and Education, 20*(2), 147–162,

Benson, K. (2000). Constructing academic inadequacy. *The Journal of Higher Education, 71*(2), 223–246.

Blad, E. (2015, May). Amid Baltimore turmoil, students and educators seek understanding. *Education Week.* Retrieved from www.edweek.org/ew/articles/2015 /05/06/amid-baltimore-turmoil-students-and-educators-seek.html

Bogdan, R. C., & Biklen, S. K. (2007). *Qualitative research for education: An introduction to theory and methods* (5th ed.). Boston, MA: Allyn & Bacon.

Bryan, J., Farmer-Hinton, R., Rawls, A., & Woods, C. S. (2017). Social capital and college-going culture in high schools: The effects of college expectations and college talk on students' postsecondary attendance. *Professional School Counseling, 21*(1), 95–107.

Camangian, P. (2010). Starting with self: Teaching autoethnography to foster critically caring literacies. *Research in the Teaching of English, 45*(2), 179–204.

Camera, L. (2015). After Baltimore rioting, Obama urges focus on education programs. Retrieved from blogs.edweek.org/edweek/campaign-k-12/2015/04/after _baltimore_riots_obama_ur.html

Cammarota, J. (2004). The gendered and racialized pathways of Latina and Latino youth: Different struggles, different resistances in the urban context. *Anthropology & Education Quarterly, 35*(1), 53–74.

Caraballo, L., Lozenski, B. D., Lyiscott, J. J., & Morrell, E. (2017). YPAR and critical epistemologies: Rethinking education research. *Review of Research in Education, 41*, 311–336.

Carey, R. L. (2016). "Keep that in mind . . . You're gonna go to college": Family influence on the college going processes of Black and Latino high school boys. *The Urban Review, 48*(5), 718–742.

Chapman, B. (2018). City to spend $23M for anti-bias training for public school educators. *New York Daily News*. Retrieved from beta.nydailynews.com/new-york /city-shelling-23m-anti-bias-training-public-schools-article-1.3956566

Colomer, S. (2018). Understanding racial literacy through acts of (un)masking: Latinx teachers in a new Latinx diaspora community. *Race Ethnicity and Education*. doi:10.1080/13613324.2018.1468749

Conklin, H. G., Hawley, T. S., Powell, D., & Ritter, J. K. (2010). Learning from young adolescents: The use of structured teacher education coursework to help beginning teachers investigate middle school students' intellectual capabilities. *Journal of Teacher Education, 61*, 313–327.

Conley, D. T. (2012). *A complete definition of college and career readiness*. Eugene, OR: Educational Policy Improvement Center.

Corasaniti, N. (2016, October 26). Donald Trump offers his version of "New Deal for Black America." *New York Times*. Retrieved from www.nytimes .com/2016/10/27/us/politics/donald-trump-black-voters.html

Costello, M. B. (2016). *The Trump effect: The impact of the 2016 presidential election on our nation's schools*. Montgomery, AL. Retrieved from www .splcenter.org/20161128/trump-effect-impact-2016-presidential-election-our -nations-schools

Crenshaw, K. W., Ocen, P., & Nanda, J. (2016). Black girls matter: Pushed out, over-policed and *underprotected*. New York, NY: African American Policy Forum, Center for Intersectionality and Social Policy Studies.

Delpit, L. (2012). *"Multiplication is for White people": Raising expectations for other people's children*. New York, NY: New Press.

Devereaux, T. H., Prater, M. A., Jackson, A., Heath, M. A., & Carter, N. J. (2010). Special education faculty perceptions of participating in a culturally responsive professional development program. *Teacher Education and Special Education, 33*(4), 263–278.

DiPrete, T. A., & Buchmann, C. (2013). *The rise of women: The growing gender gap in education and what it means for American schools*. New York, NY: Russell Sage.

Douglas, B., Lewis, C. W., Douglas, A., Scott, M. E., & Garrison-Wade, D. (2008). The impact of White teachers on the academic achievement of Black students: An exploratory qualitative analysis. *Educational Foundations, 22*(1-2), 47–62.

Durden, T., Dooley, C. M., & Truscott, D. (2014). Race still matters: Preparing culturally relevant teachers. *Race Ethnicity and Education, 19*(5), 1003–1024.

Durden, T. R., & Truscott, D. M. (2013). Critical reflectivity and the development of new culturally relevant teachers. *Multicultural Perspectives, 15*(2), 73–80.

Eskenazi, M., Eddins, G., & Beam, J. M. (2003). *Equity or exclusion: The dynamics of resources, demographics, and behavior in the New York City public schools*. New York, NY: National Center for Schools and Communities.

Expanded Success Initiative. (2012). Quick stats. Retrieved from www.nyc.gov /html/ymi/downloads/pdf/expanded-success-initiative.pdf

Farmer-Hinton, R., & McCullough, R. G. (2008). College counseling in charter high schools: Examining the opportunities and challenges. *The High School Journal, 91*(4), 77–90.

Fergus, E., Noguera, P. A., & Martin, M. (2014). *Schooling for resilience: Improving the life trajectory of Black and Latino boys.* Cambridge, MA: Harvard Education Press.

Fine, M., Torre, M. E., Burns, A., & Payne, Y. A. (2007). Youth research/participatory methods for reform. In D. Thiessen & A. Cook-Sather (Eds.), *International handbook of student experience in elementary and secondary school* (pp. 805–828). Dordrecht, Netherlands: Springer.

Ford, T. L., & Dillard, C. B. (1996). Becoming multicultural: A recursive process of self- and social construction. *Theory Into Practice, 35*(4), 232–238.

Fry, R. (2009). *The rapid growth and changing complexion of suburban public schools.* Washington, DC: Pew Hispanic Center.

Gay, G. (2010). *Culturally responsive teaching: Theory, research, and practice* (2nd ed.). New York, NY: Teachers College Press.

Gibson, M., Gándara, P., & Koyama, J. (Eds.). (2004). *School connections: U.S. Mexican youth, peers, and school achievement.* New York, NY: Teachers College Press.

Goldschmidt, H. (2006). *Race and religion among the chosen people of Crown Heights.* New Brunswick, NJ: Rutgers University Press.

Gonzales, L. D. (2012). Stories of success: Latinas redefining cultural capital. *Journal of Latinos and Education, 11*(2), 124–138.

Gonzalez, R., & Ayala-Alcantar, C. (2008). Critical caring: Dispelling Latino stereotypes among preservice teachers. *Journal of Latinos and Education, 7*(2), 129–143.

Harper, S. R. (2015). Success in these schools? Visual counternarratives of young men of color and urban high schools they attend. *Urban Education, 50*(2), 139–169.

Harper, S. R., & Associates. (2014). *Succeeding in the city: A report from the New York City Black and Latino male high school achievement study.* Philadelphia: University of Pennsylvania, Center for the Study of Race and Equity in Education.

Harris, D. (2012). *Tapping for tuition.* United States: ABC News.

Henry, A. (2017). Culturally relevant pedagogies: Possibilities and challenges for African Canadian children. *Teachers College Record, 119*(1), 1–27.

Howard, T. C. (2003). Culturally relevant pedagogy: Ingredients for critical teacher reflection. *Theory Into Practice, 42*(3), 195–202.

Jackson, I., & Knight-Manuel, M. G. (2018). "Color does not equal consciousness": Educators of color learning to enact a sociopolitical consciousness. *Journal of Teacher Education.* doi:10.1177/0022487118783189

Jackson, I., Sealey-Ruiz, Y., & Watson, W. (2014). Reciprocal love: Mentoring Black and Latino males through an ethos of care. *Urban Education, 49*(4), 394–417.

James, C. E. (2012). Students "at risk": Stereotypes and the schooling of Black boys. *Urban Education, 47*(2), 464–494.

Jernigan, M. M., & Daniel, J. H. (2011). Racial trauma in the lives of Black children and adolescents: Challenges and clinical implications. *Journal of Child & Adolescent Trauma, 4*(2), 123–141.

Kendall, F. E. (2013). *Understanding White privilege: Creating pathways to authentic relationships across race* (2nd ed.). London, England: Routledge.

Klevan, S., & Villavicencio, A. (2016). *Strategies for improving school culture: Educator reflections on transforming the high school experience for Black and Latino young men*. New York, NY: Research Alliance for New York City Schools.

Knight, M., Norton, N, Bentley, C., & Dixon, I. (2004). The power of Black and Latina/o counterstories: Urban families and college-going processes. *Anthropology & Education Quarterly, 35*(1), 99–120.

Knight, M. G., & Marciano, J. E. (2013). *College ready: Preparing Black and Latina/o youth for higher education—A culturally relevant approach*. New York, NY: Teachers College Press.

Knight-Manuel, M. G., Marciano, J. E., Wilson, M., Jackson, I., Vernikoff, L., Zuckerman, K. G., & Watson, V. W. M. (2016). "It's all possible": Urban educators' perspectives on creating a culturally relevant, schoolwide, college-going culture for Black and Latino male students. *Urban Education*, 1–30. doi.org/10.1177/0042085916651320

Kohli, R., & Pizarro, M. (2016). Fighting to educate our own: Teachers of color, relational accountability, and the struggle for racial justice. *Equity and Excellence in Education, 49*(1), 72–84.

Kozleski, E. (2010). *Culturally responsive teaching matters!* Tempe, AZ: Equity Alliance. Retrieved from www.equityallianceatasu.org/sites/default/files/Website_files/CulturallyResponsiveTeaching-Matters.pdf

Ladson-Billings, G. (1994). *The dreamkeepers: Successful teachers of African American children*. San Francisco, CA: Jossey-Bass.

Ladson-Billings, G. (1995a). But that's just good teaching: The case for culturally relevant pedagogy. *Theory Into Practice, 34*(3), 159–165.

Ladson-Billings, G. (1995b). Toward a theory of culturally relevant pedagogy. *American Educational Research Journal, 32*(3), 465–491.

Ladson-Billings, G. (2009). *The dreamkeepers: Successful teachers of African American children* (2nd ed.). San Francisco, CA: Jossey-Bass.

Ladson Billings, G. (2011). Boyz to men? Teaching to restore Black boys' childhood. *Race Ethnicity and Education, 14*(1), 7–15.

Ladson-Billings, G. (2014). Culturally relevant pedagogy 2.0: a.k.a. the remix. *Harvard Educational Review, 84*(1), 74–84.

Leonardo, Z. (2004). The color of supremacy: Beyond the discourse of 'White privilege.' *Educational Philosophy and Theory, 36*(2), 137–152.

Liou, D. D., Antrop-González, R., & Cooper, R. (2009). Unveiling the promise of community cultural wealth to sustaining Latina/o students' college-going information networks. *Educational Studies, 45*(6), 534–555.

Lipman, P. (1996). The missing voice of culturally relevant teachers in school restructuring. *Urban Review, 28*(1), 41–62.

Longsworth, K. (2018, May 11). Thank you to every teacher who shaped me into the person I am today. Retrieved from www.theodysseyonline.com/for-every-underappreciated-teacher

Lopez, N. (2012). Racially stigmatized masculinities and empowerment: Conceptualizing and nurturing Latino males' schooling in the United States. In P. A. Noguera, S. Hurtado, & E. Fergus (Eds.), *Understanding the disenfranchisement of Latino men and boys: Invisible no more* (pp. 235–254). New York, NY: Routledge.

Losen, D., Hodson, C., Keith, M. A., II, Morrison, K., & Belway, S. (2015). *Are we closing the school discipline gap?* Los Angeles: University of California Los Angeles: The Center for Civil Rights Remedies.

Lumnia Foundation (2018). *Why is the goal so urgent?* Retrieved from www .luminafoundation.org/lumina-goal#goal-urgent

Maciag, M. (2016). Immigrants establishing roots in new gateway cities. Retrieved from www.governing.com/topics/urban/gov-immigrant-friendly-cities.html

Maraj, O., Graham, A., Seetharam, N., & Williams, T. (2010). Moment 4 life [Recorded by Nicki Minaj]. On *Pink Friday* [CD]. New Orleans, LA: Young Money.

Marciano-Watson, J. (2011). *It's different when you hear it from a friend.* Retrieved from www.youtube.com/watch?v=X-ErPJ6fbx4

Marciano, J. E. (2017). "We're friends, we have to be in this together": Examining the role of culturally relevant peer interactions in urban youth's college readiness and access. *Urban Review, 49*(1), 169–187.

Marciano, J. E., & Watson, V. W. M. (2017). "Now we need to write something that people will read": Examining youth choices as perspectives of literacy research. *eJournal of Public Affairs, 6*(2), 60–85.

Martinez, M. A. (2014). College information, support and opportunities for all? *Journal of Cases in Educational Leadership, 17*(2), 94–107.

Marx, S. (2008). Popular White teachers of Latina/o kids: The strengths of personal experiences and the limitations of whiteness. *Urban Education, 43*(1), 28–67.

McClafferty, J., McDonough, P., & Nunez, A. (2002, April). *What is a college going culture? Facilitating college preparation through organizational change.* Paper presented at the annual meeting of the American Educational Research Association, New Orleans, LA.

McDonough, K. (2009). Pathways to critical consciousness: A first-year teacher's engagement with issues of race and equity. *Journal of Teacher Education, 60*(5), 528–537.

McKillip, M. E. M., Godfrey, K. E., & Rawls, A. (2012). Rules of engagement: Building a college-going culture in an urban school. *Urban Education, 48*(4), 528–556.

Melfi, T. (2016). *Hidden figures.* United States: 20th Century Fox.

Mensah, F. M., & Jackson, I. (2018). Whiteness as property in science teacher education. *Teachers College Record, 120*(1), 1–38. Retrieved from www.tcrecord .org/library (ID Number: 21958)

Miller Dyce, C., & Owusu-Ansah, A. (2016). Yes, we are still talking about diversity: Diversity education as a catalyst for transformative, culturally relevant, and reflective preservice teacher practices. *Journal of Transformative Education, 14*(4), 327–354.

Milner, H. R. (2003). Teacher reflection and race in cultural contexts: History, meanings, and methods in teaching. *Theory Into Practice, 42*(3), 173–180.

Milner, H. R. (2012). *Start where you are but don't stay there: Understanding diversity, opportunity gaps, and teaching in today's classrooms.* Cambridge, MA: Harvard Education Press.

Milner, H. R. (2015). *Rac(e)ing to class: Confronting poverty and race in schools and classrooms.* Cambridge, MA: Harvard Education Press.

Milner, (2016). A Black male teacher's culturally responsive practices. *The Journal of Negro Education, 85*(4), 417–432.

Milner, H. R. (2017). Where's the race in culturally relevant pedagogy? *Teachers College Record, 119*(1), 1–31.

Moll, L. C., Amanti, C., Neff, D., & Gonzalez, N. (2005). Funds of knowledge for teaching: Using a qualitative approach to connect homes and classrooms. In N. Gonzalez, L. C. Moll, & C. Amanti (Eds.), *Funds of knowledge: Theorizing practices in households, communities, and classrooms* (pp. 132–141). Mahwah, NJ: Erlbaum.

Monzo, L. D. (2016). "They don't know anything!" Latinx immigrant student appropriating the oppressor's voice. *Anthropolgy & Education Quarterly, 47*(2), 148–166

Moore, F. M. (2008). Positional identity and science teacher professional development. *Journal of Research in Science Teaching, 45*(6), 684–710.

National Center for Education Statistics. (2018a). College enrollment rates. Retrieved from nces.ed.gov/programs/coe/indicator_cpb.asp

National Center for Education Statistics. (2018b). Elementary and secondary enrollment. Retrieved from nces.ed.gov/programs/raceindicators/indicator_rbb.asp

National Center for Education Statistics. (2018c). Public high school graduation rates. Retrieved from nces.ed.gov/programs/coe/indicator_coi.asp

National Governors Association Center for Best Practices & Council of Chief State School Officers. (2010). *Common core state standards.* Retrieved from www.corestandards.org/ELA-Literacy/SL/11-12/

Neville, H., Gallardo, M., & Sue, D. W. (2016). *The myth of racial color blindness: Manifestations, dynamics, and impact.* Washington, DC: American Psychological Association.

Paris, D. (2012). Culturally sustaining pedagogy: A needed change in stance, terminology, and practice. *Educational Researcher, 41*(3), 93–97.

Paris, D., & Alim, H. S. (2014). What are we seeking to sustain through culturally sustaining pedagogy? A loving critique forward. *Harvard Educational Review, 84*(1), 85–100.

Paris, D., & Alim, H. S. (Eds.). (2017). *Culturally sustaining pedagogies: Teaching and learning for justice in a changing world.* New York, NY: Teachers College Press.

Paris, D., & Winn, M. T. (Eds.). (2013). *Humanizing research: Decolonizing qualitative inquiry with youth and communities.* Thousand Oaks, CA: Sage.

Pennell, S. (2016). Queer cultural capital: Implications for education. *Race Ethnicity and Education, 19*(2), 324–338.

Pollock, M., Bocala, C., Deckman, S. L., & Dickstein-Staub, S. (2016). Caricature and hyperbole in preservice teacher professional development for diversity. *Urban Education, 51*(6), 628–658.

Pollock, M., Deckman, S., Mira, M., & Shalaby, C. (2010). "But what can I do?": Three necessary tensions in teaching teachers about race. *Journal of Teacher Education, 61,* 211–224.

Ramirez, N., & Celedon-Pattichis, S. (2012). *Beyond good teaching: Advancing mathematics education for ELLs.* Reston, VA: National Council of Teachers of Mathematics.

Rodríguez, L. F. (2008). Struggling to recognize their existence: Examining student–adult relationships in the urban high school context. *Urban Review, 40*(5), 436–453.

Rogers, L. O., & Way, N. (2016). "I have goals to prove all those people wrong and not fit into any one of those boxes": Paths of resistance to stereotypes among Black adolescent males. *Journal of Adolescent Research, 31*(3), 263–298.

Rosa, J., & Flores, N. (2017). Unsettling race and language: Toward a raciolinguistic perspective. *Language in Society, 46*(5), 621–647.

Rosenberg, P. (2004). Colorblindness in teacher education: An optical delusion. In M. Fine, L. Weis, L. Pruitt, & A. Burns (Eds.), *Off White: Readings on power, privilege and resistance* (pp. 257–272). New York, NY: Routledge.

Royal, C., & Gibson, S. (2017). They schools: Culturally relevant pedagogy under siege. *Teachers College Record, 119*(1), 1–25.

Sallee, M. W., & Tierney, W. G. (2007). The influence of peer groups on academic success. *College and University, 82*(2), 7–14.

Stanton-Salazar, R. D. (2001). *Manufacturing hope and despair: The school and kin support networks of U.S.-Mexican youth.* New York, NY: Teachers College Press.

Stanton-Salazar, R. D., & Spina, S. U. (2005). Adolescent peer networks as a context for social and emotional support. *Youth & Society, 36*(4), 379–417.

Ullucci, K., & Battey, D. (2011). Exposing color blindness/grounding color consciousness: Challenges for teacher education. *Urban Education, 46*(6), 1195–1225.

Ungar, M. (2005). *Handbook for working with children and youth: Pathways to resilience across cultures and contexts.* Thousand Oaks, CA: SAGE.

Urban Institute. (2017). *Diversifying the classroom: Examining the teacher pipeline.* Retrieved from www.urban.org/features/diversifying-classroom-examining -teacher-pipeline

U.S. Department of Education Office for Civil Rights. (2016). *A first look: Key data highlights on equity and opportunity gaps in our nation's public schools.* Retrieved from www2.ed.gov/about/offices/list/ocr/docs/2013-14-first-look .pdf

Valenzuela, A. (1999). *Subtractive schooling: U.S.-Mexican youth and the politics of caring.* Albany: State University of New York Press.

Valli, L. (1995). The dilemma of race: Learning to be color blind and color conscious. *Journal of Teacher Education, 46*(2), 120–128.

Vaught, S., & Castagno, A. (2008). "I don't think I'm a racist": Critical race theory, teacher attitudes, and structural racism. *Race Ethnicity and Education, 11*(2), 95–113.

Villavicencio, A., Klevan, S., & Kemple, J. (2018). *Challenges and progress in the pursuit of college and career readiness for Black and Latino young men.* New York, NY: Research Alliance for New York City Schools.

Ware, F. (2006). Warm demander pedagogy: Culturally responsive teaching that supports a culture of achievement for African American students. *Urban Education, 41*(4), 427–456.

Warren, C., & Marciano, J. E. (2018). Youth participatory action research (YPAR) and education policy reform. *International Journal of Qualitative Studies in Education, 31*(8), 684–707. doi:10.1080/09518398.2018.1478154

Watson, V. W. M. (2016). "I don't want to say bad things about Detroit": Examining adolescent literacy as literary presence. *Michigan Reading Journal, 49*(1), 57–62.

Watson, W., Sealey-Ruiz, Y., & Jackson, I. (2016). Daring to care: The role of culturally relevant care in mentoring Black and Latino male high school students. *Race Ethnicity and Education, 19*(5), 980–1002, doi:10.1080/13613324 .2014.911169

Wells, A. S., Fox, L., & Cordova-Cobo, D. (2016). *How racially diverse schools and classrooms can benefit all students*. New York, NY: The Century Foundation.

Wiedeman, C. R. (2002). Teacher preparation, social justice, equity: A review of the literature. *Equity and Excellence in Education, 35*(3), 200–211.

Yosso, T. J. (2005). Whose culture has capital? A critical race theory discussion of community cultural wealth. *Race Ethnicity and Education, 8*(1), 69–91.

Index

The letter *t* after a page number refers to a table.

About the Authors

Michelle G. Knight-Manuel is an associate dean and professor of education at Teachers College, Columbia University, as well as a former middle school teacher and high school college advisor. Her research focuses on college readiness and access for Black and Latinx youth, immigrant youth's literacies and civic engagement, and culturally relevant education. Specifically, her research with immigrant youth deepens understandings of, and builds upon, the language and literacy practices that they bring to school. Additionally, she examines immigrant youth's notions of belonging and the potential of their civic engagement in and beyond P–16 schools as informed and active members of local/global communities. She has collaborated with teachers, school leaders, researchers, policymakers, parents/families, and community-based organizations to create more-equitable policies and practices. Her work has been published in such journals as the *American Educational Research Journal, Teachers College Record, Race Ethnicity and Education,* and the *Journal of Educational Policy.* Knight-Manuel has served on several editorial boards and is the co-author (with Joanne Marciano) of *College Ready: Preparing Black and Latina/o Youth for Higher Education—A Culturally Relevant Approach.* She is the recipient of several honors including the Spencer Foundation Small Grants Award, the American Educational Research Association's Research Service Project Award, a Faculty Research Innovation Award, and a Spencer Foundation Postdoctoral Fellowship.

Joanne E. Marciano is an assistant professor in the Department of Teacher Education in the College of Education at Michigan State University. Joanne's research engages qualitative participatory methodologies to highlight opportunities for supporting youth's literacy learning across contexts of secondary English education, teacher education, and urban education. A central part of her research agenda involves highlighting opportunities for culturally and linguistically diverse youth to examine how their schooling experiences are influenced by challenges and tensions that emerge when students encounter educational inequities. Joanne has published research findings in *Urban Education,* the *International Journal of Qualitative Studies in Education,* the *Journal of Adolescent and Adult Literacy, English Journal, The Urban Review,* and *Literacy.* She is co-author (with Michelle Knight-Manuel) of *College Ready: Preparing Black and Latina/o Youth for Higher Education—A Culturally Relevant Approach.* Joanne previously taught secondary English for 13 years in a New York City public high school.